About the Author

Samuel A. Malone is a training consultant, lecturer and author. He was previously employed as a Training Manager at the Electricity Supply Board, where he was responsible for setting up a learning centre. He is a former lecturer in Business Management at the National College of Industrial Relations (now National College of Ireland) and the author of three books, including *Mind Skills for Managers*.

SUCCESS SKILLS
FOR MANAGERS

Samuel A. Malone

Oak Tree Press

Dublin

Oak Tree Press
Merrion Building
Lower Merrion Street
Dublin 2, Ireland
www.oaktreepress.com

A catalogue record of this book is
available from the British Library.

ISBN 1 86076 139 9

Printed in Ireland
by Colour Books Ltd, Dublin

Contents

Acknowledgements...*xi*
Preface...*xiii*
List of Figures...*xvii*

1   Determination 1
    Persistence.. 1
    Stamina.. 3
    Overcoming Adversity... 4
    Overcoming Resistance... 5
    Force Field Analysis.. 7
    Planning Change.. 8
    The ASPIRE Self-Development Model 10
    Commitment to Lifelong Learning 12
    Comfort Zones... 13
    Know Your Learning Style 16
    The TRAP Model 18
    Lessons from the Learning Styles.................................... 20
    Improving Your Activist Style... 20
    Improving Your Reflector Style... 21
    Improving Your Theorist Style.. 22
    Improving Your Pragmatist Style...................................... 23
    The Four Stages of Learning... 24
    Lessons from the Four Stage Model 27
    The UNIT Model of Learning.. 27
    Lessons from the UNIT Model 29
    Summary.. 30
    Mind Map of Chapter.. 32

2   Esteem...**33**
Self-Esteem 33
Low Self-Esteem Characteristics 35
High Self-Esteem Characteristics — Positive Thinking 36
High Self-Esteem Characteristics — Learning............................ 37
High Self-Esteem Characteristics — Relationships...................... 38
Enhance Your Self-Esteem — Internal 39
Enhance Your Self-Esteem — External 40
Assertiveness and Self-Esteem 42
My Bill of Rights.. 44
The SIMILAR Model for Self-Esteem 45
Lessons from the Seven Intelligences............................. 48
Summary.. 49
Mind Map of Chapter.. 50

3   Strategic Thinking **51**
Mission, Vision and Goals 53
The Helicopter Viewpoint.. 53
The Eight Ps of Success 54
The SPEWSIC Model.. 56
Strategic Objectives... 57
Position Audit 57
Environmental Analysis 58
WOTS Up Analysis 59
Strategies to Fill the Gap 61
Strategic Models... 67
Implementation 71
Control 72
Advantages of Strategic Planning.................................... 73
The CHOICE Model 74
Summary... 75
Mind Map of Chapter.. 79

4   Communication...**81**
Importance of Communication.. 81
The PICTURE Model.. 82
The GRAPEVINE Model 83
Perception 85

Interpersonal Conflict 90
Organisational Conflict 91
Resolving Conflict 92
Conflict Styles 93
The Power of Language 95
Questions — The FLOOR Technique 99
Basic Negotiation Skills 100
Negotiation Strategies 103
Meetings 105
The Four P Agenda for Successful Meetings 107
Meetings and Group Dynamics 108
Group Roles 109
Mentoring 110
Coaching 116
Types of Interviews 119
Selection Interview 119
Counselling Interview 121
Appraisal Interview 123
The Performance Potential Model 125
Legitimate Grievance Interview 127
Disciplinary Interview 129
Summary 131
Mind Map of Chapter 135

5   **Rapport** **137**
Creating Rapport by Remembering Names 137
Matching Words 139
Watching Eye Movements 141
Matching Body Movements 141
Reframing 142
Rapport with Yourself 143
Building Trust 145
The Trust–Control Dilemma 147
The Johari Window 147
Different Strokes for Different Folks 150
Summary 152
Mind Map of Chapter 154

6   Ideals **155**
Honesty is the Best Policy 155
The Importance of Character 157
What is Ethics? 159
Stakeholder Issues 160
Common Topics for Codes of Ethics 161
The BIM Code of Ethics 162
Ethics and Power... 162
Why Ethics? 163
Survey of Ethics... 164
Monitoring Standards — The Media 166
Double Standards... 168
Positive Ethics 169
Monitoring Standards — Environmental Groups 170
Monitoring Standards — Animal Welfare 171
How is Ethics Implemented? 172
Ethics Training.. 173
Institute of Business Ethics 174
Legally Required Business Standards.......................... 175
Monitoring Standards — The Professions 176
Where is Ethics Relevant? 177
Summary... 182
Mind Map of Chapter.. 183

7   Belief **185**
The Self-Fulfilling Prophecy... 185
Fear 186
Disempowering Beliefs 187
Empowering Beliefs 188
Dream the Impossible Dream 189
The Placebo and Voodoo Effects.................................. 191
The Mind and Body are One System 191
The SAVER Model 192
Beliefs for Better Business Performance..................... 197
Integrated Nature of Beliefs and Learning................. 201
Summary... 204
Mind Map of Chapter.. 206

8   Enthusiasm **207**

    Passion 207

    Optimum Experience Model.. 209

    Faith 210

    Keeping Things in Perspective.................................... 211

    The PACE Model... 212

    Motivation.. 213

    Enthusiasm for Learning.. 215

    Summary.. 216

    Mind Map of Chapter.. 218

9   Discipline **219**

    Self-Discipline.. 219

    Internal Locus of Control.. 220

    Wisdom.. 221

    Wisdom and the Pursuit of Happiness 223

    Core Skills for Business Success 224

    The SUPPORT Model 226

    The CHARISMA Model 227

    The MISFILING Model 229

    Emotional IQ — Mind Discipline................................ 232

    Lessons from the Emotional IQ................................... 234

    Personal Financial Discipline..................................... 234

    Keep Accounts 236

    The Importance of Money.. 237

    Simplify Your Life 239

    Summary.. 239

    Mind Map of Chapter.. 242

10   Putting It All Together...**243**

    The DESCRIBED Model.. 243

    Determination 244

    Esteem... 245

    Strategic Thinking 246

    Communication 247

    Rapport.. 248

    Ideals 249

    Beliefs.. 250

Enthusiasm..251
Discipline 252
Mind Map of Chapter..255

Bibliography 257
Index..261

Acknowledgements

Tony Buzan is the creator of Mind Maps®. The term "Mind Maps®" is the registered trademark of Tony Buzan.

Many thanks to David Givens, the editor of Oak Tree Press who helped shape the manuscript into the present attractive publication.

Every attempt has been made to trace and acknowledge copyright material. The author and publisher will be happy to acknowledge copyright in future editions.

Although most of the mnemonics used in the text are my own invention, some have been acquired over the years in my role as a trainer and educationalist. If made known, I will gladly acknowledge the source of these in future editions.

This book is dedicated to my wife Veronica. Without her understanding, patience and support this book would not have come to fruition.

Preface

This book is not your usual "success" book. Instead it is a judicious mix of success psychology, neurolinguistic programming, learning principles, strategic thinking, business management and ethics. The success psychology is supported by specific business management, strategic thinking, ethics and learning to learn skills which are essential to the success of any management career. Interspersed throughout the text are inspirational stories of highly successful people. A chapter is devoted to the topical issue of business ethics and the need for sound ethical practice and its importance to the success of individuals and organisations. The chapters in this book are organised around the mnemonic DESCRIBED which is my model for personal excellence in business.

- **D**etermination is the topic for Chapter One. If you want to succeed in personal life and your business career you need determination and purpose. Winners are those who refuse to quit. To support our determination we need to be able to cope with constant change and to frequently update our skills and knowledge. With this end in view some of the best models of change and learning are discussed.

- **E**steem is the topic for Chapter Two. Our self-esteem determines how successful and happy we are in our lives. Self-esteem is one of the key characteristics of successful people. Being assertive and knowing your rights will enhance your self-esteem.

An understanding of multiple intelligence will increase our sense of self-worth.

- **S**trategic thinking. To progress to senior management positions in business you need to be able to think strategically. Knowing the SPEWSIC model is one of the key ways to help you think strategically. SPEWSIC stands for *S*trategic objectives; *P*osition audit; *E*nvironmental analysis; *W*ots up analysis; *S*trategies to fill the gap; *I*mplementation and *C*ontrol.

- **C**ommunication. Managers spend most of their time communicating. The key aspects of good communication are discussed and the importance of perception is highlighted. Good communication skills are needed in negotiations, meetings, interviews, coaching, counselling, mentoring and to deal with conflict.

- **R**apport. Rapport is a feeling of harmony with yourself and others. Being able to see things from other people's viewpoint and to empathise with them is a critical business skill. Techniques for matching words, voice and body language are discussed as well as the way of achieving harmony with yourself through reframing. Without trust it is difficult to achieve rapport with others.

- **I**deals or ethics. Many a political and business career has been ruined by an abuse of ethics. Presidents have fallen and Chief Executives jailed because of shortcomings in this regard. The importance of good ethical standards in all areas of business is discussed and the need for a company code of ethics emphasised.

- **B**eliefs. People move in the direction of their dominant thoughts. Our beliefs, values and attitudes determine what we become. You can programme your mind with positive beliefs. The core beliefs for business and personal success are explored.

- **E**nthusiasm. Do what you love and love what you do. Enthusiasm is a passion for what you do. Without enthusiasm there is little chance of true success in personal and professional life. A model is explored to show how optimum experiences can be achieved. The role of faith and motivation in enthusiasm are explored.

- **D**iscipline. The discipline of hard work and the ability to cope with disappointments are the core characteristics of successful people. The core skills for business success are discussed and a model of excellence for successful companies is explored. The reasons why companies fail are highlighted. The importance of financial discipline in business and personal life is addressed.

Chapter ten, the final chapter, brings it all together with a quick overview of the DESCRIBED model.

The DESCRIBED formula for success in personal and business life is supported by sound psychological, learning and business principles. Without the "giants" of management, success psychology, neurolinguistic programming and learning who have blazed the trail before me I would have not been able to produce this book. Some of these come readily to mind, such as Kolb, Mumford, Gardner, and numerous management theorists. I hope I have done them justice and been able to make this information available in a more digestible and relevant form for busy managers.

This book is an entertaining blend of practical tips, checklists, mind maps, acronyms, mnemonics, and success stories designed to help the reader work smarter and learn quicker. In line with good learning principles each chapter in this book begins with a list of questions and finishes with a chapter and mind map summary.

List of Figures

Force Field Analysis 8

Level of Pressure 14

Four Stages in Learning Cycle 16

Stages of Learning 25

Self-Esteem 42

Personality Characteristics 43

Product Life Cycle 68

Growth Share Matrix 69

Diffusion of Innovation Curve 71

Iceberg Model 92

The Conflict Grid 94

Performance Potential Model 126

The Johari Window 148

Five Basic Sources of Ethics 157

Why Business Ethics? 164

Unethical Behaviour Becomes Counterproductive 165

Stakeholder Theory 180

Optimum Experience Model 209

The DESCRIBED Model for Personal Excellence 244

1. Determination

"The miracle, or the power, that elevates the few is to be
found in their industry, application, and perseverance
under the prompting of a brave, determined spirit."
— Mark Twain

♦ *Why is persistence important to success?*

♦ *Why is stamina needed?*

♦ *How can you overcome adversity?*

♦ *Why is the ability to handle change important?*

♦ *What is the ASPIRE model of self-development?*

♦ *How can you use learning concepts to become more successful?*

Persistence

Successful people are determined to learn and achieve their goals. They have the willpower to stay on course and stick to the task despite setbacks and disappointments. They know that the achievement of anything worthwhile takes time. They never give up until they succeed. They discount dangers and risks and only see successful outcomes. They believe that they have all the resources they need to achieve their goals. These resources include thoughts, beliefs, values, strategies, experiences, people and possessions. These resources will be explored in later chapters.

When successful in one area of life they set themselves new goals and challenges in another. They are continually stretching themselves with new problems and opportunities. They are lifelong learners challenging their physical and mental capacities to the limit at every opportunity. Richard Branson having conquered the business world is now attempting to set new records. He nearly succeeded in being the first person in history to circumnavigate the globe in a balloon. There is a saying that when the going gets tough, the tough get going. Branson certainly shows true grit and determination. It's persistence and willpower that wins through in the end.

Calvin Coolidge said that

> nothing in the world can take the place of persistence. Talent will not; nothing is more common than successful men with talent. Genius will not; unrewarded genius is almost a proverb. Education will not; the world is full of educated failures. Persistence and determination alone are omnipotent.

There is no such thing as an overnight success!

Walt Disney was refused funding by over 300 banks before finding financial backing for his theme park idea. Margaret Mitchell's famous book *Gone with the Wind*, which was made into one of the most successful films of all time, was rejected by fourteen publishers before being published. Michelangelo spent seven years lying on his back on a scaffold to paint the Sistine Chapel. Vladimir Lenin spent thirty years preparing for his Russian revolution.

Abraham Lincoln after almost a lifetime of disappointment and setbacks eventually became President of the United States. He came from a poor background and got very little formal education. Nevertheless, he qualified as a lawyer and became one of the

United States' most famous and eloquent presidents. He once said, "I am a slow walker, but I never walk backwards."

John Hume, the Northern Ireland politician, who persistently advocated peace over more than 30 years, finally got recognition when he was awarded the Nobel Prize for Peace in 1998. Fleming worked for 16 years on the problem before he "discovered" penicillin. All of these examples show that persistence pays off in the end.

Stamina

As well as determination and commitment, successful people work hard to achieve their goals. They are not afraid of hard work and are prepared to invest long hours to achieve their ambitions. People who lack commitment will always find excuses to justify their lack of progress and aimless actions. Success has a price tag. That price tag is risk, hard work, many disappointments on the way and the expenditure of considerable time and energy. The only place where success comes before work is in the dictionary. You reap what you sow. There is no such thing as a free lunch. To quote from the Ladder of Saint Augustine:

> The heights by great men reached and kept
> Were not attained by sudden flight,
> But they, while their companions slept,
> Were toiling upward in the night.

Determined people see obstacles as opportunities to be exploited and giving up is never an issue. They don't entertain thoughts of doubt and self-pity. They refuse to quit and refuse to wallow in self-pity. The following poem was written by some unknown author but it is well worth reflecting on:

> The world won't cry if you quit
> And the world won't whine if you fail;
> The busy world won't notice it,
> No matter how loudly you wail.

Nobody will worry that you
Have relinquished the fight and gone down
For it's only the things that you do
That are worth while and get you renown

The quitters are quickly forgotten
On them the world spend little time
And a few never care that you've not
The courage or patience to climb.

So give up and quit in despair
And take your place back on the shelf;
But don't think the world's going to care;
You are injuring only yourself.

Overcoming Adversity

Overcoming adversity and obsession with personal excellence and goals are the hallmarks of determined people. Douglas Bader, Britain's war hero of World War II, lost both his legs but nevertheless became one of the most famous pilots during the Battle of Britain. Most of us with such a handicap would just give up! He was even captured but managed to escape. Milton who wrote *Paradise Lost* was blind. Helen Keller who could neither see nor hear went on to lead a very successful life. Stephen Hawking, though confined to a wheelchair and completely paralysed, is a modern Einstein. He has brought science to the layperson with the book *A Brief History of Time* which is an international bestseller.

Christopher Reeve, the actor who played the part of superman, though totally paralysed from the neck down after a horse-riding accident, puts in a day's work that would put many able-bodied men to shame. Doctors are hopeful that they may be able to regenerate the spinal cord in the future. The technique is only in its infancy and offers nothing in the way of a certain breakthrough. Nevertheless, optimism and the love and support of his wife has kept Reeve going and helped him to overcome the terrible tragedy that fate has handed him.

Some years ago a man of 65 who owned a restaurant was faced with bankruptcy. The government had built a motorway bypassing his restaurant resulting in a total collapse of sales. At that age most people would have been defeated by such a blow but he refused to quit. The only expertise he had was a chicken recipe which he decided to try and franchise. Despite many hundreds of refusals and setbacks, a few years later he had built a nationwide franchised restaurant chain called Kentucky Fried Chicken and was a millionaire into the bargain. The man was Colonel Sanders. This story proves that it is never too late to learn and it is certainly never too late to become a success in business. All you need is determination, persistence, stamina, hard work and the willpower to overcome adversity. Those who have known only success in their lives will find it very difficult to deal with failure.

Overcoming Resistance

Determined people have the knowledge to adapt and manage change. There is an old saying which is very apt in this context: "If you always do what you've always done, you'll get what you've always got". To change the results you get you must change your behaviour. You can only change yourself. You cannot change others. You can only influence by example. This point is very graphically made on the tomb of an Anglican Bishop in the crypts of Westminster Abbey:

> When I was young and free and my imagination had no limits, I dreamed of changing the world. As I grew older and wiser, I discovered the world would not change, so I shortened my sights somewhat and decided to change only my country. But it, too, seemed immovable.
>
> As I grew into my twilight years, in one last desperate attempt, I settled for changing only my family, those closest to me, but alas, they would have none of it.

> And now as I lie on my deathbed, I suddenly realise: If only I
> had changed myself, then by example I would have changed
> my family. From their inspiration and encouragement, I
> would then have been able to better my country and, who
> knows, I may have even changed the world.

In order to survive in modern business you must be able to cope
with change and turn it to your advantage. Change is a natural
part of life. The seasons change cyclically from Winter to Spring to
Summer to Autumn and back to Winter again. In life people go
through the biological cycle from birth to growth to maturity and
eventually decline and death.

> Everything flows and everything is constantly changing. You
> cannot step twice in the same river, for other waters are con-
> stantly flowing on (Heraclitus, 500 BC).

People can become more capable of handling change and more re-
silient to handling disappointment if they understand the natural
change process most people go through when they are confronted
with major change in their lives. It's a comfort to know that we all
face the same process when experiencing change. With a knowledge
of this process, managers are also in a better position to manage
change more effectively. These change stages can be described as
follows:

- *Denial*. People at first deny the change is happening. They can't
  believe that the firm will make them redundant after so many
  years loyal service. They refuse to accept reality. They are
  shocked and numb and refuse to believe their eyes and ears.
  Conflicting rumours are rife in the organisation which adds to
  their feelings of fear and uncertainty.

- *Anger*. They are angry and frustrated at the world and the organisation in particular and can't understand why it's happening to them. They feel that they are being treated unfairly and
  that the organisation has abandoned them. Their skill, status

and power base is under threat. Side by side with the anger there is a sense of loss of control and a desire to regain some control over the situation.

- *Negotiation*. They have now accepted that change is inevitable and attempt to regain some control by trying to negotiate favourable outcomes themselves or through others. Union representatives are brought in to negotiate the best deal possible in the circumstances.

- *Depression*. There is a sense of mourning at the loss suffered. They miss the companionship of fellow workers which they feel is now gone for ever. There is also fear of the unknown and concerns about the future. Negative attitudes prevail.

- *Options*. Alternatives are now considered and their consequences evaluated. The problem may now be seen as an emerging opportunity.

- *Acceptance*. People begin to adopt more positive attitudes, get on with their lives and plan for the future. After all, it's not the end of the world and life must go on.

Force Field Analysis

Force Field Analysis is a useful model as it may help a manager to identify the forces that drive and hinder change. A situation to be changed can be viewed as a balance of forces working in opposite directions: those resisting change and those driving change (see figure on following page).

Change can be brought about in two ways:

1. By increasing the strength of the driving forces, and/or

2. By reducing the restraining forces.

The length of the lines can be used to prioritise and designate the importance of the driving and restraining forces. Forcing change through by increasing the driving forces is likely to create tension, conflict and industrial unrest. On the other hand, concentrating on reducing or eliminating the resisting forces can be more successful in bringing about permanent change. This facilitates unfreezing of the old situation and the movement to a new changed situation. The final step is to freeze the situation in its new changed state.

Force Field Analysis

Restraining Forces

High 5

3

Low 1

Low 1

3

High 5

Driving Forces

Planning Change

A traditional way of planning change is to:

• Identify the problem

• Develop a plan to overcome the problem

• Inform and consult with those affected by the plan

• Implement the plan.

A more modern and effective approach to planning change is to:

- Start with the future: where you would like to be

- Consider your present state: where you are at the moment

- Consider what you need to do to get from where you are to where you want to be.

The major difference between the two approaches is that the traditional approach concentrates on the problems and the negative things that must be done to overcome them. Giving bad news to people discourages and demotivates them at the very time that their morale needs to be kept up. On the other hand, the modern approach encourages positive thinking by concentrating on the desirable vision and goals achievable in the future. People are motivated by goals which mobilises their imagination, enthusiasm and commitment. So as a manager you must make the future goal exciting and desirable for the critical mass of your staff if you want to win acceptance for change.

In summary, to handle change successfully a manager should:

- Start with the future. Concentrate on the desirable future state. Paint the future as a vision of a prosperous and successful company.

- Draw up action plans and programmes to get you from the present position to the future state. Predict the potential difficulties and plan to overcome them.

- Earn trust and credibility by being honest and up-front about the whole change process. Keep the staff informed and get them fully involved as partners in the change programme. Consult unions, if appropriate.

- Exude confidence and commitment to the change process in order to win the confidence and commitment of others. You are a role model for staff. If you don't "walk the talk", they won't!

- Implement an effective communications programme. Listen to, empathise, and deal with the concerns of employees.

The ASPIRE Self-development Model

Determination must be combined and supported by a vision, goals, plans and action programmes. Determination without purpose is unlikely to bring you success in your career. Careers need to be planned and not left to chance. The mnemonic ASPIRE will help you remember the required steps for a successful self-development plan:

- **A**ssess your current position. Decide where you are now. Decide your future desired state: where you want to be. Consider how you can get there. Successful people think about missions, roles, values, visions and goals. A mission is discovering the purpose of your life. A role is the various identities you have to assume to achieve your mission. Values are what is important to you. Vision translates our life purpose into images specific enough to inspire. The conflict between the vision and the reality of your present position drives you forward. Your subconscious generates the energy to achieve the vision. Goals are the specific results you want to achieve in order to fulfil your mission. Once you set a goal the reticular activating system in the brain heightens your awareness to new information which will help you achieve your goal. This is why when you decide to do research on a particular topic you suddenly begin to see sources of information and ideas for your topic all around you. The goals should be consistent with your values. There is a big difference between having a dream and becoming a success. Not all dreamers achieve but all achievers are dreamers. Remember Martin Luther King's famous speech: "I have a dream"? Successful people support their dreams with action. Success comes to those people who dream things and then take the necessary practical actions to make their dreams come true.

- **S**WOT analysis. SWOT stands for strengths, weaknesses, opportunities and threats. Strengths might include your positive attitude, experience, qualifications, and good IQ. Weaknesses might include your tendency to be reactive and to procrastinate. An opportunity might be an offer of promotion while a threat might be the possibility of company closure. Carry out a strengths and weaknesses analysis of your capabilities. Try to turn weaknesses into strengths and threats into opportunities. Notice the gap between your existing level of experience and knowledge and the desired level. Consider what you need to do to fill it. This might include further experience, training and educational qualifications. Write down your long-term and short-term targets.

- **P**lan. Draw up an action plan to achieve your long-term and short-term goals. In the long term you may need to do an MBA or professional qualification to give you the competitive edge and help you get ahead in the future. In the short term you may need to develop all-round computer expertise such as word processing, database, spreadsheet and graphical presentation skills. Consider the resources you'll need to acquire to support your plan. Resources would include finance, equipment, knowledge, skills and support from others.

- **I**mplement. Decide the *steps* to be taken and the *deadlines* that will make things happen realistically. Reduce it to manageable (daily/weekly) steps. Focus your concentration by doing one thing at a time. Edison, probably the greatest inventor of all time, and who patented over 1,000 commercial products including the electric light bulb and gramophone, always concentrated on one thing at a time. Write daily to do actions into your diary. Tick them off as you achieve them. This will concentrate your mind, give you a sense of accomplishment and satisfaction, and help motivate you to continue.

- **R**eview. Write down the rewards (immediate, intermediate and final) to yourself when you have achieved your goals and sub-goals. What will you feel, hear and do on the achievement of your goals? What praise, compliments, recognition and respect will you earn? See yourself graduating with that MBA! Imagine the scene and sense the elation. Feel the pride of the occasion. A combination of desire, imagination and expectancy will keep you going and see you through in the end.

- **E**valuate. How successful have you been in achieving your personal development goals? What can you learn from any setbacks or mistakes? What corrective action do you need to take to put things right and get you back on target again? Evaluation is a continuous process against sub-goals until your desired end-goal is achieved.

Commitment to Lifelong Learning

These days a commitment to lifelong learning is essential for success in any career. The days when you could progress in your management career on the sole basis of on-the-job performance are long gone. The days of getting ahead on the basis of who you know rather than what you know are disappearing fast. Today you are expected to have a primary degree and/or professional qualifications and often post-graduate degrees as well. It was Henry Ford, the great innovator of the modern car who said: "Anyone who stops learning is old, whether 20 or 80. Anyone who keeps learning stays young. The greatest thing in life is to keep your mind young." There are always new challenges in life and something new to learn.

Adult learners often have negative attitudes about formal learning situations which hold them back. These have been inherited from unhappy experiences during their time in school. However, you can change your attitude. It was William James who said that "the greatest discovery of my generation is that a human being can alter his life by altering his attitude of mind".

To counteract negative attitudes to learning the learning environment should be supportive and non-threatening. Managers do most of their learning on the job and this environment should also be supportive and non-threatening. The blame culture should be avoided and mistakes seen as learning opportunities rather than occasions for recrimination. Learning on the job and off the job should be fun, never boring, threatening or judgemental. In fact, learning is more effective when its challenging and fun to do. Learners should be reassured that the learning will be easy, relaxing, useful and enjoyable.

Comfort Zones

To learn anything you must move out of your comfort zone. Comfort zones are areas of thinking and experience to which we confine ourselves so as not to feel threatened, uneasy or "out of our depth". Personal development comes from venturing beyond and expanding our comfort zones. People who succeed take risks and welcome new personal development opportunities. John F Kennedy said: "There are risks and costs to a programme of action. But they are far less than the long-range risks and costs of comfortable inaction".

Progress and growth are impossible if you always do things the way you've always done them. Being stuck in a rut will not help you advance in your career. First weigh up the considerations and then take the risks. Try and learn new things each year. Set yourself personal challenges daily. Continuous personal development and improvement should be your goal.

Do new things occasionally. Take up new challenges. Accept that lateral transfer even if there are no immediate monetary rewards. It will broaden your experience, reactivate your mind and put you in a stronger position for promotion in the future. Study new sub-

jects for mental challenges and stimulation. Reading is a great way
of keeping your brain in shape.

The following diagram illustrates the difference between the
comfort zone, the stretch zone, the strain zone and the panic zone.
Your objective should be to move smoothly from the comfort zone,
where you are underachieving, to the stretch zone, where you fulfil
your true potential. This is attained by being committed to the task,
not being afraid to take appropriate risk, while at the same time
having a balanced approach to work and recreation. On the journey
from the comfort zone to the stretch zone it is important not to get
side-tracked into the panic or strain zones.

Level of Pressure

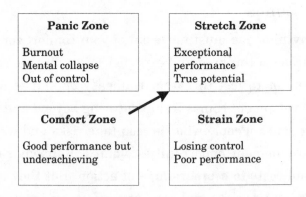

The Comfort Zone

This is where you feel most comfortable. It offers you challenge and
stimulation without being overstretched. You are not under pressure and feel comfortable with your life. You won't get ulcers in the
comfort zone but neither will you do anything exceptional. You need
challenges from time to time to keep you on your toes. You can ex-
pand your comfort zone by the use of imagination and visualisation.
Practise in your mind the new behaviours that you want to adopt.

This will prepare your mind to get used to the idea of the new comfort zone.

The Stretch Zone

This is the zone which takes you out of your comfort zone. It offers challenge and you begin to feel some pressure. In this zone you will learn more, acquire new skills, increase your self-esteem and self-confidence and equip yourself to take on even more challenging work. In the stretch zone you have the energy and confidence to keep going. This is the zone you're in when learning new skills such as project management or PC skills. Sometimes it is referred to as the "flow" zone.

The Strain Zone

Here you are overstretched and losing control. Work no longer gives you satisfaction and your performance deteriorates. You begin to experience a lot of stress. You need to nip the problem in the bud before it gets out of control by putting balance back into your life. Moving too far outside your comfort zone results in decreased effectiveness and poor performance. Take some time off for rest, recuperation and relaxation.

The Panic Zone

Here you are stressed out and feel you can't cope. Something snaps and you feel overwhelmed. You are easily irritated and argumentative. Your colleagues may notice this decline but you may be completely unaware of the problem. Some executives drive themselves into this state and may finish up in a complete state of burnout and mental collapse.

Know Your Learning Style

Effective learners are aware of their learning style. If you know your particular learning preference then you are in a better position to improve and compensate for shortcomings in your less dominant styles of learning. In line with the philosophy of continuous self-improvement, learning is a cyclical process. This means you go through the same stages again as ever increasing levels of skills and knowledge are attained. David Kolb identified the four stages in the learning cycle as experience, reflection, theorising and experimentation. These are shown in the diagram below:

Four Stages in Learning Cycle

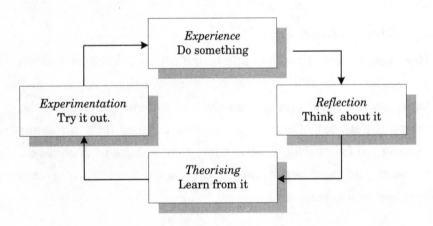

- **Experience (activist).** Learning by experience takes place on the job every day. In the world of work it is the most common type of learning and sometimes the only type of learning that many employees get. Most of a manager's learning comes through the experience of working in the real business world. There is no comparable substitute for the "hands-on approach". Hence the popularity of on-the-job training such as secondment, mentoring and project work. In a formal training situation case studies, role play, demonstrations and simulations are often used to try and model the real-life world of work. However, true learning does not take place until you reflect on it, understand its significance and integrate it into your own internal world. This brings us to the next stage of learning.

- **Reflection (reflector).** This means just thinking about your experiences. G.B. Shaw was reputed to have said: "Most people do not think, I have made a fortune from thinking about once or twice a week". Take a few minutes at the end of each day to mentally review what you did during the day and what lessons can be learnt from your experience. Visualise the activities of the day in images and pictures. What would you have done differently if you had the opportunity all over again? Keep a learning log to record, review and learn from your experiences. Henry Ford is reputed to have said that thinking is the hardest work there is, which is probably the reason why so few do it. Thoughtful reflection on past experience with a view to improve in the future is a key learning experience.

- **Theorising (theorist).** Relate your experience to theoretical models or indeed develop your own concepts or models. These will act as guides in your future actions. How does the practice differ from the theory? In the world of business abstract models are just that — abstract! It is unlikely that what actually happens bears any resemblance to the theory. Nevertheless we may develop principles, policies, guidelines and our own conceptual models to help us manage more effectively in the future. Unless we learn from our past we will fail to make progress in the future. This brings us to the next stage of the cycle.

- **Experimentation (pragmatist).** This means trying out your ideas. You are exploring, discovering and finding out what works and what doesn't work. If something doesn't work you try something else until you get the desired results. This feedback channels your energies and determination in a positive and constructive way. This will enable you to solve problems and make decisions. After this the learning cycle starts again and continues its indefinite cycle. The learning cycle is thus a cycle of continuous feedback of learning and relearning.

The TRAP Model

People have different approaches to learning. Some people are inclined to be academic and are interested in theories and concepts. Others are more interested in the practical side of things. Adult learners in general like to get involved actively in their own development, like to have a say in the running of their own jobs, to share their ideas and experiences and to be self-directing and problem-centred. Some learners are more left-brain dominant while others are more right-brain dominant. This means that some people are analytical and rational and prefer logical and sequential learning experiences. Other people are creative and artistic and like plenty of interaction, visual experiences and role play.

To develop our brainpower we should engage in a variety of learning experiences. These should appeal to both the rational and artistic parts of the brain and to as many of our senses as possible. In particular, the visual (see), auditory (hear) and kinaesthetic (feel) senses should be catered for. For a visual learner, a picture speaks louder than a thousand words. Educationalists now believe that we learn 10 per cent of what we read, 15 per cent of what we hear but 80 per cent of what we experience.

Alan Mumford and Peter Honey (1997) have identified four types of learners. The four types can be identified by the mnemonic TRAP which stands for Theorist, Reflector, Activist and Pragmatist. These can be linked to the learning cycle as shown above.

- Theorist. Theorists tend to be detached, logical, analytical and rational. They are keen on basic assumptions, principles, theories, models and systems thinking. They feel uncomfortable with ambiguous experiences, creativity and lateral thinking. They like to organise different facts into coherent theories. They are good people to have around because of their objectivity. In a group situation they may come up with interesting factually-based alternatives and challenge the conventional wisdom. Theorists make good system analysts.

- **Reflector.** Plato said that "the life which is unexamined is not worth living". Reflectors tend to think deeply about their experiences and consider them from different viewpoints. They like to consider the facts before they come to a conclusion. They tend to be cautious and have the philosophy of "look before you leap". At meetings they seem to be quiet and detached but are good listeners. Part of their approach is to get as many different points of view as possible before making up their own minds. They like to think and reflect. The Lord gave us two ends — one to sit on and the other to think with. Success depends on which one we use the most! Reflectors make good strategic planners.

- **Activist.** As the name suggests, activists enjoy getting things done. They are very much involved in the here and now. They enjoy learning new experiences. They tend to be reactive rather than proactive. They thrive on crisis management. They enjoy brainstorming and lateral thinking. They are gregarious, attention-seeking and like to be the life and soul of the party. They are more at home in operational management rather than a strategic role.

- **Pragmatist.** As the name suggests these people have a very practical bent. They can't wait to try out ideas, theories and techniques to see if they work in practice. They are the type of people who come back from course programmes bursting with ideas and very keen to apply them. They see problems as opportunities and threats as challenges. They know that there is a better way of doing things. They believe in the philosophy of continuous improvement. Pragmatists make good computer programmers.

Lessons from the Learning Styles

Most people will have a mix of the four learning styles with a preference for one or two. You can determine your learning styles by taking Honey and Mumford's learning styles questionnaire which takes about 20 minutes to complete and is very reliable for determining particular learning styles.

It is important to find out your learning preferences so that you can take corrective action on your weaker styles. Also, when selecting people for jobs, it might be a good idea to find out what particular learning style they prefer in order to place them into suitable roles. Some jobs place emphasis on certain learning styles rather than others. For example, general managers tend to be pragmatists and activists rather than reflectors and theorists. On the other hand, people in strategic planning and research and development would need to have strong reflector and theorist styles.

In a job where decisions have to be made quickly it is unlikely that a reflector and theorist style would be suitable. On the other hand, in a strategic planning role these styles would be essential for success. In a training situation a course programme should be designed to appeal to the four learning styles or in certain cases to the preferential learning styles of participants if that is known. It would be a good idea to get course participants to do a learning styles questionnaire before a course programme to ascertain their individual learning styles. Managers should do likewise before they coach their staff. The following are based on Honey and Mumford's ideas on how to improve the various learning styles.

Improving Your Activist Style

- Do something new. Visit a part of your organisation which you haven't seen before. Talk to different functional specialists about their roles. Join a society which deals with matters outside your current experience. Take a different route to work.

Change newspapers occasionally to get a different perspective on current affairs. Try out a new restaurant, preferably one from a different culture. Visit a museum at lunchtime. Don't always wait for other people to take the initiative; do things first yourself! When you are buying a new car, go for a different make this time rather than sticking to the same manufacturer all the time.

- In social situations and at conferences, introduce yourself first. At the supermarket check-out, exchange some friendly words with the check-out operator. Become more involved in your professional institute. Get involved in a political party and go door-to-door canvassing for your favourite parliamentary candidate.

- Change activities during the day. If you have been working hard take some time off for reflection and meditation. If you tend to be quiet and reserved, take the initiative at meetings by asking appropriate questions. On the other hand, if at a meeting you find yourself doing a lot of the talking, take some time off to listen and reflect — you may learn something.

- At professional institute meetings put yourself forward for officer positions such as chairperson, secretary, public relations officer or education officer. These bodies are always looking for volunteers and such positions can be great learning, developmental and social opportunities.

Improving Your Reflector Style

- At meetings become an observer of human behaviour. Study people's body language such as posture, voice, gestures, eye movements, expressions and reactions. Look for hidden agendas and see how disagreements are resolved. Spend some time inside your own head by thinking and reflecting on situations. In general, develop a philosophy of reflecting before you jump into a situation or arrive at conclusions.

- Keep a learning log. Record your learning experiences at the end of each day and reflect on the lessons which can be learnt and applied in the future. See mistakes as learning opportunities rather than mini-disasters. Remember that your goal is continuous improvement and self-development. Those who cannot remember the past are condemned to repeat it. Unfortunately, too many managers today ignore the past. Consequently, by failing to reflect on it they let valuable learning lessons escape which would enhance their development and performance in the future. Managers should review their successes and failures, assess them systematically and draw lessons from them for application in the future.

- Do some in-depth research on a topic that interests you. Go to the library and ask the librarian for guidance. They are usually only too willing to help. Visit your local bookshop and see what are the latest publications on the subject. Invest part of your income in building up a good library. Broaden your interest by learning a new subject each year.

- Practise looking at issues from three perspectives: your own, the other person's and a detached viewpoint. Consider the case for and against. Write the points down and reflect on the issues involved. Try and draw an impartial conclusion based on the facts of the case. Do not ignore intuitive feelings about the issue as these can sometimes be right.

Improving Your Theorist Style

- Read academic books on management and organisational development. Summarise each chapter in the form of a mind map. Keep these for reference and review occasionally. Study well known theoretical models in management such as the Product Life Cycle, the Growth Share Matrix, Maslow's Hierarchy of Needs, Blake and Mouton's Managerial Grid and Likert's Four Systems of Management.

- Look for flaws in other people's arguments. Study reports critically for illogical statements and to see what unsupported conclusions are arrived at and what inconsistencies arise. Study books critically to see what is factually based and what is mere opinion. Study systems and procedures in your workplace to spot unnecessary tasks, inefficient operations and duplication. Study forms to see if they can be improved by combination, re-arrangement or elimination of unnecessary requirements.

- Develop a questioning approach to problems. Seek out the reasons for company policies and procedures by continually asking the reason "why"? You'll surprise yourself occasionally by discovering that there is no logical basis for some policies and procedures.

- Plan your week by drawing up schedules and your day by preparing to do lists and keeping a diary.

Improving Your Pragmatist Style

- Develop expertise in a wide variety of practical management techniques. Examples would include critical path analysis, flow charts, decision trees, force field analysis, cause and effect diagrams, breakeven analysis, variance analysis, ratio analysis, pareto analysis, discounted cash flow and cost benefit analysis. Set yourself the objective of learning one technique per week. Become aware of the strengths and weaknesses of these techniques and determine the areas of work in which they can be applied.

- Collect self-developmental techniques such as problem solving, assertiveness, presentation skills, memory skills, speed reading skills, transactional analysis, neurolinguistic programming and so on. These will broaden your mind and contribute substantially to your professional development. Look for opportunities to attend courses on these topics.

- Model yourself on successful people. Model their voice, words, gestures and beliefs and attitudes. President Clinton openly admits that he modelled his presidential style on that of President Kennedy. You can become successful yourself by modelling the success strategies of successful people.

- Ask a trusted colleague for feedback on your presentation skills, interpersonal relationship skills, meeting skills or work performance. Look for constructive criticism. Remember that mistakes are learning opportunities and you can improve outcomes by reflection and changing your behaviour.

- Tackle do-it-yourself projects around the house rather than getting others to do it. Take on that repair job yourself. Become your own interior designer. Paint and wallpaper your home. Develop PC expertise such as word processing, spreadsheet analysis, data bases and graphical presentation skills.

The Four Stages of Learning

Awareness of how you learn will make you a more competent learner and a more successful and committed person. All learning involves persistence, determination and disappointments on the way. Psychologists have discovered that there are four stages in learning which progresses from unconscious incompetence to conscious incompetence to conscious competence and lastly unconscious competence (see figure on following page). Let's now look at each of these stages in some detail.

Stages of Learning

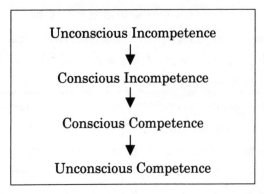

Unconscious Incompetence
↓
Conscious Incompetence
↓
Conscious Competence
↓
Unconscious Competence

Unconscious Incompetence

This is the stage of learning where you don't know that you don't know. You are just not aware of your own level of ignorance and lack of experience. If you've never driven a car you will have no idea of what is involved. For example, very young children, like my own 6-year-old grandson, often imagine they can drive a car. Their confidence exceeds their ability. If you have ever given driving lessons you begin to appreciate just how much of your knowledge and skill is unconscious. This is why it is so difficult for an experienced, competent driver at the unconscious competent level to train somebody at the unconscious incompetence level. Their skills have become habitual automatic responses and are thus very difficult to verbalise, organise and explain consciously. Many a happy marriage has come to grief because one partner has agreed to teach the other how to drive without really thinking about how difficult and traumatic it can prove to be. This demonstrates just how much of our everyday actions are done unconsciously with the minimum of conscious awareness on our part. Everyday habits are activated unconsciously.

Conscious Incompetence

This is the stage of learning where you know you don't know. To learn new things you must move out of your comfort zone. You start to learn how to drive. Your confidence drops when you see how awkward you are. You feel you would need to be an acrobat to co-ordinate the movements required for steering, clutch, brake and accelerator while at the same time watching the control dials and the road. This is the stage where you have kangaroo starts, grind the gears, jerky stops, oversteer and generally challenge the patience of your instructor and other road users. You learn most at this time but need confidence, persistence and determination to take you to the next stage. Motivation, encouragement, goals, action plans and taking responsibility for your own learning will get you there in the end. Some people get frustrated and lose confidence at this stage and give up. Consider the number of people who start educational programmes, pay their money and shortly afterwards give them up at great financial loss and personal inconvenience. They don't realise that everybody goes through the same stages of the learning curve and experience similar feelings, frustrations and difficulties. There is no gain without some pain. Determination will see you through in the end.

Conscious Competence

This is the stage where you can drive the car but you are very conscious of the fact. It takes all your concentration and energy. However, your confidence increases in line with your skill. You are proficient but not a master of the art. You may even pass the driving test at this stage but you must make a conscious effort to reach the required standard. Overconfidence may be a problem leading to the taking of unnecessary risks. The result of this is a high rate of accidents for newly qualified young drivers which is confirmed by road accident statistics.

Unconscious Competence

At this stage you can drive, learn educational tapes, listen to the radio and converse at the same time. Some drivers even manage to converse on their mobile phones while driving although this practice is not recommended and is illegal in some countries. The movements involved in driving the car have become an automatic response. Your unconscious mind has taken over the routine, freeing your mind to concentrate on the rules of the road and the prevailing traffic conditions. Driving has become a habit. However, the problem with habits is that there are bad habits or poor practice as well as good habits. Many a person over the years has unconsciously acquired poor driving habits which may need to be eliminated and replaced by good habits. This process can be facilitated by unlearning stages 4 to 2 and relearning stages 2 to 4.

Lessons from the Four Stage Model

Expertise in any area of life takes time, determination, persistence and commitment. It will take about 10 years of application and reading before you become an expert in any subject. Learning is a process not a destination. To learn you must go from unconscious incompetence to unconscious competence.

The journey of a thousand miles begins with a single step. As soon as you attain mastery you must keep up to date with developments and best practice as well as consolidating and practising your existing skills. If you fail to do so your knowledge will be forgotten or become out of date. It is a question of using it or losing it. Lifelong learning and continuous self-improvement is the name of the game. The leading professional bodies have taken this concept on board through their continuing professional development programmes which are mandatory in some cases.

The UNIT Model of Learning

The four types of learning can be recalled by the mnemonic UNIT which stands for Unlearning, New learning, Incremental learning and Transformational learning. Knowing about these will help you to understand and categorise the types of learning you are currently involved in.

- **Unlearning.** These days many old ways of doing work have to be unlearned and new ways substituted for the old. The old learning habits die hard and often interfere with our new learning. When changing your old car for a new model you often have to unlearn old habits and learn new ones for improved controls and layouts. With PCs new and updated programmes come out all the time where learnt commands of previous versions, which have gone into our long-term unconscious memory, often give new unexpected results or indeed new commands must be learnt to get the same results. Most of us are reluctant to unlearn what we know. In unlearning you must drop existing knowledge which is now redundant to make room for something new.

- **New learning.** In new learning you will go from a state of unconscious incompetence to a state of unconscious competence. You will go through an "S" curve of progress where after an initial slow period of learning, you will make rapid progress until you come to a plateau. At this point it is important to stick to the task as eventually you will progress to a higher plain of learning. New learning is hard work and requires determination and persistence for success. Repetition and practice is needed to consolidate the new learning.

- **Incremental learning.** This means building on your existing learning. For example, you may be already fairly competent in making presentations. Many people stop here and don't bother to pursue excellence. However, you can always improve by adopting an attitude of continuous improvement. There is always room for doing better and there is always more to learn about any particular job. Maybe the organisation of your presentation could be improved by having a better introduction and a more positive conclusion. In between you might use your tone, pitch and delivery to create interest and variety. Being competent in one Windows-based software package means you can transfer the knowledge to another Windows-based package and learn it quite easily.

- **Transformational learning.** This is called a paradigm shift. This is possibly the most important type of learning because it changes your whole perspective, system of beliefs and attitudes. In creative thinking it is the "Aha!" experience when you suddenly see things in a different light. For example, you may see your job as a great source of satisfaction rather than a mere source of money. Galileo's discovery, published in 1632, that the sun, not the Earth was the centre of the universe and that the Earth moved around the sun and not vice versa is a good example of a paradigm shift. In modern times, business process re-engineering is a radical redesign of business processes to achieve dramatic improvement in productivity and efficiency. It is planned transformational learning.

Lessons from the UNIT Model

Unlearning old ways of doing things and learning new methods is part and parcel of modern living. The old learning often interferes with the new learning but with practice this will fade away. New learning goes through the natural stages of unconscious incompetence to conscious competence. Nothing worthwhile is learnt overnight; so be prepared for the long haul!

Incremental learning is possibly the most common type of learning we engage in. It is also linked to the idea that nothing stays still and we need to continually update and improve our skills. Vegetate and you die.

Transformational learning is radical and the type of learning that you need sometimes to cope with discontinuous change. People often have to go through dramatic changes of belief, culture, attitudes and skills training in order to progress. Information technology and business process re-engineering often gives rise to the need for transformational learning.

Summary

If you want to succeed in life and your business career you need determination and purpose. You also need an attitude of not giving up too easily. Winners are often those who refuse to quit. Successful people are energetic and need stamina for the long hours invested over many years to achieve worthwhile goals. Change is a constant factor in modern society and an understanding of the change process will help us to cope more effectively. The ASPIRE model for self-development was discussed. ASPIRE stands for:

- Assess current position

- SWOT analysis

- Plan

- Implement

- Review

- Evaluate.

The TRAP model for different types of learners was highlighted. TRAP stands for:

- Theorist

- Reflector

- Activist

- Pragmatist.

To cope with constant change we need to be able to frequently update our skills and knowledge. Thus determination to succeed needs to be accompanied by a strong desire for lifelong learning. To equip you for this task an awareness of the latest thinking in learning such as the types of learning, learning stages model, the learning cycle and styles of learning will prove to be very useful in your search for personal excellence. The various types of learning can be recalled by the mnemonic UNIT. This stands for:

- Unlearning
- New learning
- Incremental learning
- Transformational learning.

Determination, purpose and lifelong learning are some of the essential ingredients for a successful career.

Chapter 1 Mind Map

1. DETERMINATION

Traits
- Persistence
- Stamina
- Adversity
- Resistance
- Overcoming

Change
- Force Field Analysis
- Planning

Self-Development
- Current Position
- Assess
- SWOT
- Plan
- Implement
- Review
- Evaluate
- ASPIRE
- Lifelong Learning
- Comfort Zones

UNIT Model
- Incremental
- Transformational
- New Learning
- Unlearning

Learning Stages
- Conscious Incompetence
- Unconscious Incompetence
- Conscious Competence
- Unconscious Competence

TRAP Model
- Theorist
- Reflector
- Activist
- Pragmatist

Learning Styles
- Experience
- Reflection
- Theorising
- Experimentation

2. Esteem

*"Until you value yourself you will not value your time.
Until you value your time, you will not do anything
with it." — M. Scott Peck*

*"Low self-esteem is like driving through life with the
hand break on." — Maxwell Maltz*

♦ *What is self-esteem?*

♦ *What are the characteristics of high self-esteem people?*

♦ *How can you enhance your self-esteem?*

♦ *How important is assertiveness to self-esteem?*

♦ *What is the SIMILAR model for self-esteem?*

Self-esteem

Self-esteem is the value you place on yourself. It is a feeling of confidence in your abilities to achieve desirable goals. It means liking
or feeling good about yourself, your appearance or your abilities. If
you don't value yourself nobody else will. Your self-esteem determines how effective and successful you are in your life. It has
nothing to do with IQ or fame. Many people with high IQ suffer
from low self-esteem. Many famous people resort to alcohol and

drug abuse to bolster up poor self-esteem. Psychologists believe that there is a strong correlation between self-esteem, your sense of well-being and your capacity for self-development and true success in life. Managers with low self-esteem lack confidence and do not believe in lifelong learning and thus never reach their true potential. Unfortunately, they often stifle the development of their staff as well. High self-esteem means a willingness to take risks, to respond to challenges and seek out opportunities for learning and self-development.

People with high self-esteem are less frequently sick, generally live longer, recover quicker from illness and have enhanced immune systems. They have a positive outlook on life, are content and happy and have a high sense of self-worth. The body and mind are interlinked. One affects the other.

Self-esteem can be specific. In some areas of our lives we may feel high self-esteem, whereas in other areas we may have feelings of low self-esteem. For example, as a training consultant I feel high self-esteem or confidence in the training room. On the other hand, I feel less confident at parties or social occasions. Obviously, we feel confident about areas in which we are very proficient while we lack confidence in those areas where we show less skill. Our objective should be to minimise overexposure to those areas in which we feel a sense of low self-esteem. If we lack confidence in certain areas which are critical to our jobs then we should make it our business to become proficient in those areas.

Self-worth is associated with self-respect and is an important aspect of self-esteem. Self-worth is your overall sense of value, worth and a belief that you are making a worthwhile contribution to society. Your sense of worth can change over time, based on your actions, job, sense of achievement and position in life. For example, my sense of self-worth has increased over time as I:

• Gradually learned to be a responsible parent and husband

- Helped others through my writing, lecturing and training consultancy

- Gained modest recognition through my published books.

Low Self-esteem Characteristics

- People with low self-esteem resist change and feel threatened by it.

- They tend to be critical of themselves and others. They adopt an attitude of "beggars can't be choosers".

- They maintain their own status by devaluing and running down others. They are usually reactive rather than proactive.

- They are self-centred rather than empathetic.

- They expect frustration, lack of fulfilment and problems rather than positive outcomes.

- They visualise the penalties of failure rather than the rewards of success. They find it hard to accept praise and compliments.

- They are out of control rather than in control of their lives.

- They pursue and expect immediate gratification. This often leads to self-destructive behaviour such as smoking, eating and drinking too much, abusing drugs and driving too fast.

- They resist new learning opportunities because they fear the possibility and shame of failure.

- They are risk-averse. They do not realise that if you do what you've always done you'll get what you've always got. If you want to get different outcomes you've got to change your behaviour and do different things.

- Because they blame and complain a lot of people find it difficult to work with them. People like working with happy, positive people. People prefer working with people they like. Thus we tend to avoid moaners and groaners.

High Self-esteem Characteristics — Positive Thinking

- People with high self-esteem practise positive self-talk and like themselves. This does not mean that they are conceited or full of self-importance. On the contrary, they accept their limitations and have a realistic view of their own strengths and weaknesses. This sense of self-acceptance or feeling comfortable about yourself is an important aspect of mental health. Self-acceptance is an acknowledgement of one's own inherent self-worth. Many psychologists believe that self-acceptance is the first step to the mastery of our lives. Self-accepting people are prepared to throw themselves into all kinds of activities which lead to self-expression and possibilities of personal growth.

- They think positively. This positive thinking is expressed through positive language. One reinforces the other. They focus their minds on the things and resources they have rather than on what they do not have. They concentrate on the good things in life rather than the bad. It was Norman Vincent Peale who said that there is a basic law that like attracts like. Negative thinking attracts negative results. Conversely, if a person habitually thinks optimistically and hopefully, their positive thinking sets in motion creative forces — and success tends to flow towards them.

- They believe that they are capable of achieving success in whatever form they desire it. You don't have to be rich and famous to be happy and successful. Success is not equated with status or wealth but with contentment and balance in life. Success is 80 per cent attitude and 20 per cent aptitude.

- They have an abundance mentality rather than a famine mentality. They adopt the attitude of "the world is my oyster". They don't begrudge others fame and fortune because they realise that there is plenty to go around.

- They tend to be happier, more self-confident and decisive, less fearful or doubt-ridden and more likely to achieve success than are negative thinkers. They tend to see the humorous side to life.

- They believe that hard work is its own reward and that success will come to those who work for it. They realise that there may be many disappointments on the road to success.

High Self-esteem Characteristics — Learning

- People with high self-esteem enjoy doing new things, take calculated risks and are eager to accept new challenges and exploit new opportunities. The Chinese character for "crises" is made up of two pictograms; one represents "danger", the other "opportunity". In a group situation they are the first to volunteer to take on new tasks.

- They display a positive can-do attitude. They see possibilities rather than constraints and limitations and what's right about a situation rather than what's wrong. There is no failure only feedback. Thus they see problems as challenges to be overcome and mistakes as learning opportunities.

- They are solution-centred rather than problem-centred. Thomas Edison, the great American inventor, used to say: "From the time a child starts play school to the time he graduates from college, he will be examined three or four times a year, and if he fails once, he's out. Now an inventor fails 999 times, and if he succeeds once, he's in. An inventor treats his failures like practice shots."

- They are open to new learning opportunities, and believe in the concept of lifelong learning, continuous self-development and improvement.

- They are aware that the subconscious mind can't tell the difference between a real experience and one that is vividly imagined. They thus know that it is possible to programme the mind for success in any area of life whether in one's career or in learning.

- They articulate, visualise and emotionalise their affirmations which are in the present tense, personal, clear, specific and positive.

High Self-esteem Characteristics — Relationships

- They surround themselves with positive happy people and avoid negative grumpy people. This reinforces their positive approach to life. Their self-esteem becomes a self-fulfilling prophecy.

- They enjoy meeting new people and find it relatively easy to win the love, respect and friendship of others. They practise empathy and try always to view problems from different perspectives.

- They use self-to-self comparisons and concentrate on their successes not failures. Comparisons with others are invidious and lead only to envy, jealousy and resentment. Steward B. Johnson said: "Our business in life is not to get ahead of others, but to get ahead of ourselves — to break our own records, to outstrip our yesterday by our today."

- They accept praise and compliments by saying "thank you".

Managers who have high self-esteem, think positively and promote high standards of achievement and self-esteem in their staff. They encourage their staff to plan their careers and develop themselves for future promotion. To be successful in life, self-esteem and positive thinking in itself is insufficient. It must be backed up with goals and action plans and the commitment and energy to make it happen.

Enhancing Your Self-esteem — Internal

To enhance your self-esteem we must mainly focus on change from within. Winners use constructive self-talk like: "I want to;" "I look forward to"; "I'll do it". Losers say: "I can't;" "I'll try"; "I'm not good enough". The following are some practical tips to increase your self-esteem:

• Constantly use positive affirmations and self-talk. Remember the mind can't hold two thoughts at the same time; so make sure the thought you hold is positive and constructive rather than negative and destructive.

• Walk tall and at a relaxed but reasonable pace. A confident posture suggests a positive mind. On the other hand, a slumped posture is often seen as a sign of stress or interpreted as a lack of self-esteem and confidence.

• Be yourself, feel good about yourself and have a high sense of self-acceptance and self-worth. After all, you are truly unique. On conception you were the sperm out of 200 million which combined with one particular egg. You won the first race of your life to survive. You are a winner from the beginning.

• Recall and visualise times when you were successful and felt confident and good about yourself. Visualise by seeing a movie in your mind's eye and replay it frequently. Use an anchoring technique to associate into this state of past high self-esteem when you need to do so. An anchoring technique triggers off a reaction. For example, a Vietnam veteran may dive to the ground upon hearing a car backfire. You may instantly recall a school event upon hearing a bell. Anchors can occur naturally or be set up intentionally. A favourite piece of music may act as your anchor. Jack Nicklaus and other golfers use visualisation to enhance their game. They rehearse every shot in their imagination before going on the golf course. Olympic gold medalist diver Greg Louganis used visualisation as part of his preparation for every dive.

- Audit your strengths and weaknesses. Maximise your strengths and minimise your weaknesses. Turn threats into opportunities and weaknesses into strengths. Target areas in which your self-esteem needs building. Put into operation a self-improvement plan to rectify the situation. See yourself moving gradually but decisively towards the accomplishment of your goals. Visualise what you will see, hear and feel when you achieve them.

- Accept the things you cannot change and change the things you can. Don't expect everyone to like you. You can please some of the people all of the time, and all of the people some of the time but you can't please all of the people all of the time. Remember the Serenity Prayer by Reinhold Niebuhr: "God, give us grace to accept with serenity the things that cannot be changed, courage to change the things which should be changed, and the wisdom to distinguish the one from the other".

- Use the "as if" technique — act as if your are already feeling high self-esteem in a situation where you want this to be the case.

- Reframe situations where you experienced low self-esteem. Re-interpret situations in a more favourable light so that you feel good about them.

Enhancing Self-esteem — External

- Be well-groomed and dress your best. First impressions do count. It takes about four minutes to make a first impression. In these four minutes 55 per cent comes from the clothes you wear, 38 per cent comes from body language and tone of voice and only 7 per cent from what you say. You are judged initially to a large extent by your grooming and appearance. If you look good you'll feel good about yourself and others will feel good about you. A positive mindset is translated into positive behaviour and positive reactions towards you.

- Sit up front in seminars. This says you're enthusiastic and eager to learn. You'll also get a better view of what's going on.

- Set your own standards — self-to-self comparisons. Don't compare yourself with others. You are unique. Benchmark yourself against your own aspirational standards. In the marathon everybody who finishes gets a medal and you compete against yourself.

- Volunteer your name when meeting people for the first time and use their name frequently in conversation. There is no sweeter sound to a person than the sound of their own name. Remembering names will help you make friends.

- Model the behaviour of high self-esteem people. Study the beliefs, attitudes, words and body language of confident people and associate into how it feels to be them.

- Exercise regularly. Research shows that people who exercise regularly have a better self-image than those who don't. They are also less likely to suffer from anxiety or depression and are better able to cope with stress. Exercise programmes have helped people diagnosed as clinically depressed. They have also helped older people to improve memory as well as keeping reflexes and reasoning sharp.

A simple diagrammatic representation of self-esteem might look like this:

Self-Esteem

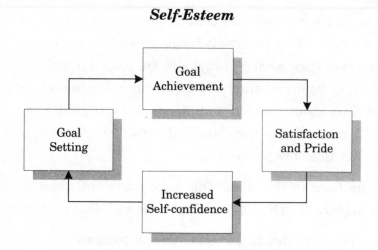

Achieving targets leads to positive outcomes which leads to satisfaction and pride which in turn leads to increased confidence and self-esteem. It's the self-fulfilling prophecy in action.

Assertiveness & Self-esteem

People with high self-esteem are assertive. There is a difference between being passive, aggressive and assertive. Being passive or non-assertive means:

- Having difficulty standing up for oneself. Letting people "walk all over you." You are not a doormat.

- Voluntarily giving up responsibility for yourself and handing it over to others who may not have your interests at heart. They certainly are unlikely to put your interests ahead of their own.

- Encouraging persecution by assuming the role of victim or martyr. In transactional analysis, this is known as the game "kick me": manipulating others into hurting or punishing you.

Being aggressive means:

- Standing up for your rights in such a way that other's rights are violated.

- Being self-enhancing at the expense of others by putting them down or humiliating them. This may include using past wrongs, imagined or real, as an excuse to hurt another.

- Antagonising others by hostile or offensive words or deeds.

On the other hand, assertiveness means being able to express your needs, preferences and feelings in a way that is neither threatening, unmannerly nor harmful to others:

- Without causing undue annoyance, fear or anxiety

- Without violating the rights of others

- Without demeaning the value of others.

Assertiveness means direct, honest communication between individuals interacting equally and taking responsibility for themselves. Assertiveness is about choice and having respect for yourself without losing respect for others. Unfortunately, double standards often operate, e.g. women who are assertive are often seen as aggressive and unfeminine while assertiveness in men is seen as a sign of strength and confidence.

Personality Characteristics

Body Language	Aggressive	Passive	Assertive
Voice	Loud	Low	Firm
Speech	Fast	Slow	Normal
Language	Strong	Hesitant	Positive
Tone	Abusive	Apologetic	States needs
Body	Tense	Slumped	Erect
Gestures	Strong	Fumbling	Stands/sits still
Movement	Towards person	Shrinking away	Normal distance
Eye Contact	Eye to eye	Avoiding	At a slight angle

In summary, assertiveness means:

- Respecting yourself

- Taking responsibility for your actions

- Recognising your own needs and accepting that they're as important as anybody else's

- Making clear "I" statements

- Allowing yourself to make mistakes. After all people learn from their mistakes

- Allowing yourself to take pride in your successes without being pompous or arrogant

- Accepting that changing your mind is not a sign of weakness but sensible in certain circumstances

- Asking for "thinking it over time"

- Asking for what you want

- Respecting other people's rights.

My Bill of Rights

This is a well-known charter for people who want to be assertive. It is based on democratic principles. I have the right to:

- State my own needs

- Be treated with respect

- Express my feelings

- Have and give my own opinions

- Say "yes" or "no" as appropriate

- Make mistakes

- Change my mind

- Say that I don't understand

- Ask for what I want

- Refuse to take responsibility for the problems of others

- Deal with others without being dependent on them for approval

- Run my own life.

The SIMILAR model for self-esteem

In his book *Frames of Mind* (1984), Howard Gardner gives seven reasons to boost our self-esteem. We are all intelligent in our own unique way. The challenge is to find the way. In this book he identifies seven different types of intelligences which we all have to a lesser or greater degree. The difference between successful people and lesser mortals seems to be the extent to which successful people are able to build up particular abilities often by sheer enthusiasm, willpower, effort and years of training. Also, they are often helped by being in the right place at the right time. These intelligences can be recalled by the mnemonic SIMILAR which stands for **S**patial, **I**nterpersonal, **M**usical, **I**ntrapersonal, **L**inguistic, **A**nalytical or logical and **R**eflex or movement abilities.

Spatial. People with spatial intelligence are good at objects and shapes, charts, diagrams, pictures and maps. Well-known examples would include Pablo Picasso, Rembrandt, Leonardo Da Vinci and Michelangelo. People with this ability are excellent at visualisation and think and remember things in the form of pictures. Graphic artists, architects and navigators have this ability. To enhance this ability use mind maps, diagrams, graphs, flow charts and your powers of visualisation. Of course, successful people with this innate ability working in the professions have, in addition, long years of training and practice behind them.

Interpersonal. These people are good at interpersonal relationships. They have a good sense of empathy and get along very well
with others. Well-known examples would include Diana, Princess of
Wales, and TV personalities Oprah Winfrey and Terry Wogan.
They tend to be extroverts. Salespeople, trainers and human resource people such as interviewers, counsellors and negotiators
need this ability to survive in their jobs. To enhance this ability get
involved in teams, debating societies, teach others, engage in small
talk with shop assistants and socialise as much as possible.

Music. Mozart obviously enjoyed this ability to an exceptional degree. Most of the rest of us exercise this talent to a lesser extent by
listening to music and singing along to a tune. Composers, song
writers, musicians and pop artists have this ability. Beethoven,
Elton John, The Beatles, Frank Sinatra and Elvis Presley would be
prime examples. To enhance this ability relax to music and study or
read to Baroque music playing softly in the background.

Intrapersonal. These people tend to be introverts. In the learning
styles model they are called reflectors. They tend to be introspective,
focusing on inner feelings and intuitions. Monks and others in the
religious life tend to have developed this ability to a high degree.
Freud's science of psychoanalysis emerged from his great capacity for
introspection. Jung classified people as introverts or extroverts.
Writers, philosophers and psychologists need this ability to be successful in their careers. Well-known examples would include Plato,
Aristotle and Socrates. To enhance this ability reflect on your life's
experiences on a daily basis and record them in a diary.

Linguistic. These are people who are good at reading, writing,
talking and languages. They tend to have a good vocabulary, be flu-
ent speakers and good all-round communicators. Your ability in
this area is likely to increase right through life and into your fifties,

sixties and seventies. Poets, writers, actors, preachers and politicians tend to have highly developed linguistic skills. William Shakespeare, Winston Churchill, John F Kennedy and Bill Clinton would typify linguistic intelligence. This skill is highly valued in most occupations and in life generally. Many politicians have this ability to a high degree. To enhance this ability learn from books, tapes, lectures and seminars. Do crosswords and debate issues with friends. Take up part-time lecturing or join Toastmasters.

Analytical or logical. People with this intelligence are good at logic, problem-solving and mathematics. Accountants, actuaries, engineers, scientists and lawyers are some of the professions that value this ability. In everyday life, people good at household budgeting, organising and time management have this ability. It is usually noticed early in life and peaks at between 30 and 40 years of age. Like linguistic ability, it is highly valued in the academic and business world.

Reflex or movement. This is also called kinaesthetic intelligence. Athletes, racing drivers, dancers, mime artists and gymnasts all have kinaesthetic intelligence. Surgeons and the skilled trades also need this ability. Surgeons need fine-tuned kinaesthetic skills to carry out operations and skilled tradespeople need highly developed manual skills. Well-known examples would include Thomas Edison, Michael Flatley, George Best, Charlie Chaplin and Muhammad Ali. People with this ability have a hands-on approach and tend to be mechanically-minded. Experiential learning enhances this ability. The action learning approach to management development uses this intelligence. Role play to act out what you are learning will also use this intelligence. To enhance this ability, take notes, make models, learn on the job and practise. The importance of practice to success was emphasised by Gary Player who is reputed to have said "the more I practise the luckier I get". Practice makes perfect.

Lessons from the Seven Intelligences

The theory of multiple intelligences is a cause for celebration and high self-esteem. It seems we all have plenty of ability if only we make the commitment and action plans to exploit our unique talents. You can integrate the seven intelligences into your self-development and continuous improvement plan. When studying you can summarise your work in the form of mind maps, flow charts and diagrams. This is an application of spatial intelligence. You can discuss issues in groups or get involved in project work. This is an example of interpersonal intelligence. You can relax to your favourite music. This is an example of musical intelligence. Inventing jingles and rhymes to help you remember critical issues is another example.

Reflecting on your work on a daily basis is an example of intrapersonal intelligence. Can you learn from your mistakes and would you do things differently in the future? Keeping a learning log would be a formal way of reviewing. Better still, get involved in a learning set that systematically goes through the learning cycle of reviewing and reflecting on actions taken at work, drawing conclusions and trying out new ideas.

Writing and making presentations to other managers is an example of linguistic intelligence as is brushing up on your French and German skills by attending night classes. Inventing mnemonics as memory joggers will improve your linguistic intelligence and ability to recall. Getting involved in the preparation of your departmental budgets or flow-charting organisational systems is an application of logical intelligence.

Lastly, the hands-on approach to work such as developing PC skills and training schemes such as job rotation are examples of the development of kinaesthetic intelligence. In your social life, playing sport of any kind such as soccer or tennis will enhance this ability.

Analyse your seven intelligences and find opportunities to develop those that at present are underutilised and that could help you progress further in your career. Jobs such as accountancy and engineering develop your logical skills to a high degree. It might be a good idea to balance these with any opportunities to develop linguistic and interpersonal skills that are essential for general management.

Conventional IQ tests concentrate on logical and linguistic abilities and are a poor barometer of success in the business world where other abilities such as hard work, determination and enthusiasm are just as important if not more so. IQ tests gave rise to the notion that intelligence was fixed at birth and that IQ was the sole criterion of intelligence. This is not true. We all have the ability to improve our multiple IQ. It just takes a lot of dedication and effort.

Summary

Our self-esteem determines how successful and happy we are with our lives. Self-esteem is one of the key characteristics of successful people. The characteristics of people with high self-esteem were explored in some detail. Being assertive and knowing your rights will enhance your self-esteem.

You can take positive action to enhance your self-esteem by practising some of the strategies suggested. The multiple intelligence theory suggests that each of us has a wide range of potential abilities — all the more reason why we should have high self-esteem. It's really a question of exploiting these natural gifts. The SIMILAR mnemonic will help you remember the seven intelligences:

- Spatial

- Interpersonal

- Musical

- Intrapersonal

- Linguistic

- Analytical

- Reflex.

Chapter 2 Mind Map

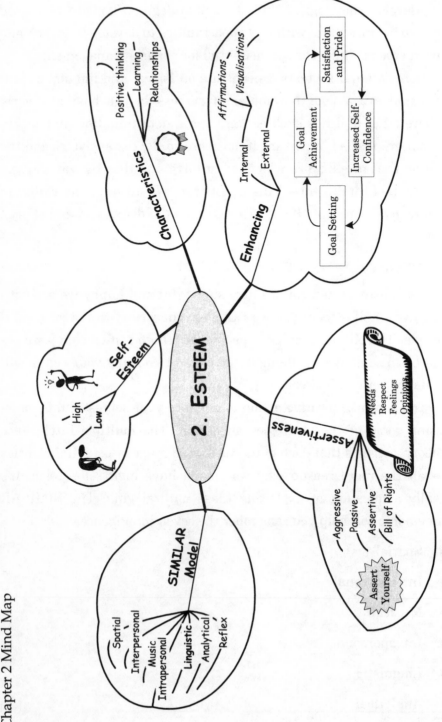

3. Strategic Thinking

*"Management's job is to see the company not as it is . . .
but as it can become." — John W. Teets*

*"One day Alice came to a fork in the road and saw a
Cheshire cat in a tree. 'Which road do I take?' she asked.
'Where do you want to go?' was his response. 'I don't
know,' Alice answered. 'Then,' said the cat, 'it
doesn't much matter.'" — Lewis Carroll*

- ◆ *What is strategic thinking?*

- ◆ *What is the helicopter viewpoint?*

- ◆ *What are the eight Ps of successful business?*

- ◆ *What is the SPEWSIC model of strategic thinking?*

- ◆ *What is the CHOICE model for thinking?*

- ◆ *What are the strategic models?*

Strategic thinking is a systematic approach to clarifying long-term objectives, making strategic decisions and checking to see what progress has been made to achieve the objectives. Strategic thinking is essential to success in a senior management position. It separates those who are destined for higher things in management from those who are going to remain in the same middle management position for the rest of their lives. In practice, it has been found that most senior managers, including company directors, are reactive rather than proactive and spend most of their day on operational issues. Their mindset often finds it difficult to accommodate the reflective and conceptual thinking needed for strategy. They often feel that if they are not "busy" they are not doing their jobs properly. Thinking about the future is too unsettling and uncertain, especially when you have real live operational issues to deal with right now!

Strategic thinking is proactive in that it is concerned with planning for the future and tries to anticipate the type of problems that may have to be overcome in order to achieve the aims of the organisation. Strategic thinking is concerned with external issues such as customers, competitors, suppliers, markets, technology and finance.

Lower levels of management are concerned with tactical and logistical matters, the short-term and medium-term problems facing the organisation. Senior managers are concerned with the long-term survival of the organisation.

Some organisations do not believe in strategic planning. The opposite to strategic planning is called freewheeling opportunism. This is where opportunities are exploited as they arise, judged on their individual merits and not within the rigid structures of strategic planning. The believers in freewheeling opportunism see this approach as flexible and adaptable and consider strategic planning a straitjacket constraint discouraging entrepreneurship, creativity and initiative. However, freewheeling opportunism may fail to consider all the opportunities and focus on profits only without taking the broader picture into account such as stakeholder needs.

Mission, Vision and Goals

Strategic thinking is the type of long-term thinking that senior managers involve themselves in when deciding the long-term future of the organisation. Mission, vision and goals are often talked about in that order. A mission has been defined as a general objective, often visionary, often unwritten, and very open-ended, without any time limit for its achievement. A vision is an inspirational mental image of the future we strongly desire. The vision translates the mission into images specific enough to focus our attention on.

The goals are more specific and should be capable of measurement. What are the fundamental goals of the organisation and where does it want to be in, say, five years' time? In the meantime, what decisions does the organisation need to take to achieve its goals? In formulating goals the company must take the needs of stakeholders into account. Stakeholders are the various groups of people who have a stake in what the company does. Shareholders own the business, but there are also lenders, suppliers, managers, workers, the government, local community and customers. Each of these groups has its own objective, so that a compromise or balance needs to be achieved. Management must balance the profit objective with the pressures from the non-shareholder groups in deciding the strategic targets of the business.

The Helicopter Viewpoint

"Paralysis by analysis" is a description of the type of manager who gets bogged down in detail. On the other hand, the helicopter viewpoint is the ability to see the big picture. It is the ability to stand back and see the big issues in a problem and not be sidelined by minor details. Pareto analysis is a well-known management technique which will help you develop the helicopter viewpoint. It was Russel Palmer, former dean of the Wharton School of Business in the US who said: "The good leader is always a person who sees the big picture, and keeps focusing their organisation on those major objectives, refusing to allow them to get bogged down with insignificant details."

The helicopter viewpoint is the type of ability which senior managers should possess in abundance. It is the type of thinking that managers at the top of an organisation are paid to do. It is a skill which separates strategic thinkers from operational thinkers. However, unfortunately research suggests that many senior managers are firefighters rather than strategic thinkers. People displaying an ability to think strategically in their early careers are often earmarked for fast-tracking to senior management positions.

The Eight Ps of Success

This stands for Purpose, Plan, Passion, Principle, Product, Position, Profit and People. Attention to these will ensure the success of the organisation.

- **Purpose**. An organisation needs a mission, vision, and clear corporate objectives. If you don't know where you're going you're likely to finish up somewhere else. The mission statement tends to be quite broad and sets out the basic reason for the existence of the organisation in terms of customers and markets. The mission is supported by the vision statement which is an inspirational mental image of the future that the organisation strongly desires. The vision statement should inspire, motivate and focus the energies of employees on the achievement of goals. Goals tend to be more specific and measurable and should be aligned to the vision.

- **Plan**. The plan gives the organisation a sense of direction. Plans can be strategic, tactical or logistical. The strategic plan is for the long term up to five years or more. The tactical plans are the annual business plans and budgets and the logistical plans are the daily, weekly and monthly schedules needed to keep the business going. As the saying goes, failing to plan is planning to fail.

- **Passion**. This is the driving motivational force which an owner/manager usually displays. Consider the passion displayed by Henry Ford when pursuing his dream of providing an automobile which the masses could afford and Richard Branson when setting up his airline and music business empire. This passion often disappears as the organisation gets bigger, formal systems are put in place and the pivotal role of the original founder diminishes. Nevertheless, it can be rekindled by inspirational management, divisionalised structures, empowerment and innovative reward systems.

- **Principle**. This is the philosophy and ethos of the company as expressed in ethical and customer service statements. It can be seen in the way a company deals with its employees, customers, suppliers and how it responds to its competitors. If a company doesn't treat its employees well then it can hardly be surprised if the employees in turn do not treat customers well. A company should be seen to be fair and honest in its dealings with others. These days the standard of ethics in many companies leaves a lot to be desired. This is supported by numerous newspaper reports of financial scandals in organisations dealings with customers and the taxation authorities.

- **Product**. Obviously, to be successful in business you need to provide a top class product or service offering value for money to your customers. If you don't, in a competitive market, customers will go elsewhere until their needs are satisfied. Quality now is more or less assumed. Many customers are now more concerned with good customer and after sales service.

- **Position**. You need to differentiate your product or service in relation to your competitors. Customers will only buy from you if you're offering something special. Advanced technology, superior design, prompt delivery, credit terms, loyalty schemes and customer service are just some of the ways you can differentiate your product or service in relation to others.

- **Profit**. At the end of the day you can't survive without profit and a healthy cash flow. Many businesses go bust not through lack of profits but through lack of cash. Profit on its own is not sufficient if the profit is tied up in unsaleable stock, debtors and bad debts. As the old rhyme goes:

    Turnover is vanity
    Profit is sanity
    Cash is reality

    High sales are often a sign of overtrading rather than profitability. Overtrading is the expansion of the production and sales of the business without adequate financial support.

- **People**. Without a committed and highly motivated workforce you are unlikely to succeed in business. People are your greatest resource. In a learning organisation people are appreciating assets, unlike capital assets which are depreciating. Investing in people through learning, training and development is investing in intellectual capital.

The SPEWSIC Model

This is a mnemonic which stands for **S**trategic objectives, **P**osition audit, **E**nvironmental analysis, **W**ots up analysis, **S**trategies to fill the gap, **I**mplementation and **C**ontrol. It covers the basic strategic planning process. In practice, the sequence of this model may not be rigidly followed.

Strategic Objectives

These answer the question "Where do you want to be in, say, five years' time?" Mission and vision statements and corporate objectives should be formulated. Objectives can be at corporate, departmental, sectional or individual level. At individual level they are usually expressed through management by objectives programmes. Drucker said that the primary objective of a company was to create a customer. However, the creation of customers should be linked to profitability. Secondary objectives can relate to social, ethical, environmental, employee and technological issues.

Position Audit

The position audit answers the question where are you now and what resources do you have? Sometimes this is referred to as a capability profile. The resource audit can be grouped under the eight Ms as follows:

- *Manpower* or human resources, including areas like size of workforce, education, experience, skills, costs, productivity, training, morale and industrial relations.

- *Materials*, including sources, cost, stock control and wastage. You can't afford to be dependent on a single supplier who may go bust. Doing business with a variety of suppliers instead of one reduces risk. This is the portfolio concept in action.

- *Money or financial issues*, such as sources of finance and the debt/equity ratio. A company with a high debt in relation to equity is said to be highly geared and has a high exposure to financial risk in the form of interest and loan repayments. A company with a low debt in relation to equity is said to be lowly geared and has a low exposure to financial risk. It is also in a better position to raise long-term loans if needed for expansion.

- *Machines and capital equipment* — their value, age and replacement time. Review your manufacturing capability and resources. If your capital equipment is out of date, have you the necessary finance to replace or upgrade it?

- *Management profile*. The size of the team, their age profile, experience, education, training and development and management succession needs.

- *Marketing*. This would include customers, orders, competitors, advertising, market research, market share and market growth. At what stage of the product life cycle is your product? If it is at the decline stage have you new products in the pipeline to replace it?

- *Management structure and culture*. The way the company is organised and its value and belief systems. Has it a bureaucratic or organic structure? What is the prevalent leadership style within the company? An autocratic style of management may not be suitable for a modern progressive organisation.

- *Management information systems*. The types and effectiveness of MIS systems. It is impossible to run a modern business without good MIS systems. You need MIS systems for all areas of your business, including production, marketing, personnel and finance.

Environmental Analysis

This answers the question: "What type of environment will the company be operating in?" A good way of classifying the types of environments can be recalled by the mnemonic PEST which stand for:

- **P**olitical and legal. Political issues include changes in government policy, including nationalisation, deregulation and privatisation. Legal issues include the regulatory framework for business, including company, mercantile law, employment law and tax laws.

- **Economic, competitive and marketing.** Issues here include changes in interest rates and foreign exchange rates. Is the economy in a boom, stable or recessionary phase? Competition includes the threat from existing competitors, the threat from new entrants, the bargaining power of suppliers, the bargaining power of customers, and the threat from substitutes. Marketing issues include the profile of customers and market conditions, whether the market is in decline, stable or increasing.

- **Social, demographic, ethical and ecological.** Social conditions include unemployment, early retirement, corporate social responsibility and increases in the service sector for employment. Demographics is the movement in population trends. Ethical issues include equality, sexism, safety, and how the company behaves in the community. Ecological issues relate to disposal of toxic waste, oil pollution, noise pollution and having respect for the environment.

- **Technological.** This refers to the technology of products and services and also the technology involved in the production process. Robotics, automation, telecommunications and the PC revolution are topical technological issues.

Wots Up Analysis

This is a variation on SWOT. SWOT stands for strengths, weakness, opportunities and threats. SWOT analysis answers the question: "What are your strengths and weaknesses and what are the opportunities and threats facing the organisation?" The strengths and weaknesses aspect is sometimes referred to as the internal appraisal or strategic advantage profile. This should be done in relation to your competitors. The threats and opportunities aspect is sometimes called the external appraisal or the external threats and opportunities profile.

The internal appraisal looks at:

- *Corporate image and culture.* Do you have a positive image with the general public? What sort of a culture do you have?

- *How efficiently and effectively have resources been deployed?* These would include manpower, materials, money and machines.

- *The management leadership style and organisation structure.* Is your leadership style and organisation structure in line with a progressive organisation in a modern economy? Or is it bureaucratic and out of date?

- *The products/service sold.* Is your product of a high standard and technologically advanced? Does it offer value for money?

- *Sources of finance and the debt/equity ratio.* What is the best financial structure for your company? What is the optimum mix of long-term debt and ordinary shares?

- *Capital equipment.* Is your plant and machinery up to date and in line with the best of your competitors? When is it due for replacement?

- *Research and development.* How effective is your R&D in producing successful commercial products?

- *Employee profiles.* What is the age, experience, education and training profile of your employees?

The external appraisal looks at:

- *Customers and markets.* Who are your customers and what type of market do you operate in? Have you adopted a customer orientation philosophy?

- *Sources of supply*. Who are your suppliers and how reliable are they?

- *The economy*. Is the economy in boom, stable or recessionary phase?

- *Technology*. What are the latest developments with your particular technology? How do you compare with your competitors?

- *Government policy*. What is government policy in relation to environmental issues, taxation and to your industry in general?

- *Competition*. Who are your competitors and what strategies are they likely to pursue in the future? Have you benchmarked your performance against the best of your competitors?

- *Social trends*. What changes in lifestyle, demographics and preferences are likely in the future? What impact will this have on your business?

Gap analysis is the technique used to compare the existing position with the desired position as regards profits, sales, human resources, facilities, return on capital employed and earnings per share. By identifying the gap you are then in a position to decide what strategies you need to undertake to fill the gap.

Strategies to Fill the Gap

These are the things a company must do to meet its corporate objectives. There are a whole range of strategies which can be undertaken, including organic growth, acquisition, marketing and business strategies.

Organic Growth Strategies

Organic growth strategies are:

- *Market penetration*. This is where the company tries to increase its market share of current markets with current products, e.g., through competitive pricing, advertising, sales promotion, spending more on distribution or direct selling.

- *Market development*. This is where the company seeks new markets for its current products, such as exporting when the company has previously served only the domestic market.

- *Product development*. This is where the company seeks to create new products to replace existing ones, for current markets and through existing distribution channels.

- *Diversification*. This is where the company seeks to develop new products in new markets. This is the strategy with the greatest risk.

Acquisition Strategies

Acquisition strategies include:

- *Horizontal diversification*. This occurs where a company takes over competitors in the same line of business. Considerable synergy should be achieved here in all aspects of the business. This would arise if two banks decided to merge or if one bank took over another. It is a quick way of increasing the size of markets, the range of products or services and customer base of the business.

- *Vertical diversification*. This can be of two types: backward vertical integration and forward vertical integration. An example of backward vertical integration would be where an oil distribution company gets involved in oil refining and exploration. Forward vertical integration would be where an oil company involved in oil refining moves into retail distribution as in petrol filling stations. A company which is totally integrated has control over its sources of supply and distribution channels. This strategy reduces risk because of the greater control you have over the inputs and outputs of a business.

- *Concentric diversification*. This occurs when a company tries to seek to add new products that have technological and/or marketing synergies with the existing product line. These products will normally appeal to new classes of customer. For example, a motor manufacturer may decide to make farm machinery. There is a technological similarity between the two, although the type of customer will be different. Some synergy might be expected in production and marketing. Another example is Saab, the Swedish motor company, which manufactures cars and aeroplanes. There are technological synergies between the two products.

- *Conglomerate diversification*. This consists of making entirely new products for new classes of customers. These new products have no relationship to the company's current technology, products or markets. There may be some management synergy where the company's managers are already experienced in running a conglomerate group of companies. An example of conglomerate diversification would be the move by a crystal glassware manufacturer into department stores, stationery and garages. This is what Waterford Glass did in the past but has since divested these companies. A conglomerate strategy is often considered risky. Hence the emphasis these days of getting back to the core business.

Marketing Strategies

Marketing mix strategies include:

- *Product*. A product means anything offered to a market for its use or consumption. It can be a physical product or a service. The range of products offered by a company is called a product mix. This could be a range of cars or a range of chocolate bars.

- *Price*. Price is the amount of money that a product or service sells for. Cost, competition and strategy are some of the factors which determine price. Price is a common method of differentiation. In terms of price, a company may decide to operate in the top part of the market or the lower part.

- *Promotion*. Promotion is any marketing activity designed to sell a product or service. It includes advertising, direct marketing, personal selling, sales promotion and publicity.

- *Place*. This means the sales outlets and distribution through which the product or service gets to the final customer.

The company must decide what aspects of the marketing mix yields the best results for money invested.

Other marketing strategies include:

- *Market share strategies* — building, holding, harvesting and withdrawal. Building is an aggressive strategy to build up market share. Holding is a defensive strategy to hold on to market share. Harvesting is allowing market share to fall to earn better short-run profits. Withdrawal or divesting is pulling out of the market.

- *Market segmentation*. This is the subdividing of a market into distinct subsets of customers. Such subsets may be selected as a target market to be reached with a distinct marketing mix.

- *Market positioning* is where you position the product in the market as a prestige product or value for money product.

- *Differentiation*. This is where you differentiate your product or service from competitors in relation to price, packaging, quality, design, brand, customer service or distribution channels.

Business Strategies

Business strategies include:

- *Strategic alliances*. This is where two companies agree to co-operate on some specific activity but otherwise remain separate entities. It might involve sharing expertise such as co-marketing, co-production or joint research and development. Such co-operation may increase efficiencies and increase market share. Airlines, telecommunications companies and car manu-facturers have formed strategic alliances in the past.

- *Joint ventures*. A venture undertaken to supply a specific serv-ice or product by two companies. A joint venture may be attrac-tive to an American or Japanese company seeking to get a foot-hold into EC markets in co-operation with a local company.

- *Franchising*. This is where trademarks, know-how, exclusivity and management assistance are provided for a down payment, royalties and adherence to company standards. Following the American Civil War (1861-1865) Singer Sewing Machines was one of the first firms to set up an international distribution sys-tem by giving a franchise to dealers. Well-known examples to-day would be McDonalds and Prontoprint.

- *Leasing*. Companies may lease capital equipment instead of purchase. This conserves cash flow and may provide some tax advantages. There are two types of leasing — an operational lease and a financial lease. In an operational lease ownership remains with the lessor whereas in a financial lease it usually passes to the lessee. In the case of a financial lease, the cost of the asset must be shown as a fixed asset on the lessee's balance sheet. In the case of an operational lease, the cost is in the form of rental payments in the profit and loss account and is not shown in the balance sheet.

- *Licensing*. This strategy involves giving another company a license or permission to use its technology or other expertise. A licence is usually taken out for patented inventions and innovations. In return, the owner of the licence receives a royalty. Licensing offers a quick way of getting increased sales and international distribution with minimum risk and investment.

- *Mergers*. A merger is the voluntary coming together of two separate companies to form a single company. On the other hand, an acquisition is the purchase of a controlling interest in another company. Mergers are often the preferred method of diversification because they provide access to new technology, management expertise, sources of supply and markets. Corporate indigestion occurs when a merger results in an unhappy marriage with diseconomies of scale arising instead of economies of scale. This may be caused by the clash of two different company cultures.

- *Divestment* occurs where a company sells off a part of its operations, or decides to pull out of certain product-market areas which are no longer profitable. It may be a strategy of cost reduction by getting back to the core business.

- *Management buyouts*. This is a form of demerger in which the managers of a subsidiary company buy it out. The managers put in some of their own capital (usually part of redundancy settlements), but get the rest from banks or the company they're buying from and hope to make a bigger success of the business than the company who is selling it off.

- *Corporate venturing*. This is a strategy option for large companies who wait for new products to emerge from small companies. They may invest in these companies and buy out the company when the product has been sufficiently developed and shows favourable signs of success. This avoids some of the risk involved in the research and development of your own product.

Strategic Models

Models which might be used to help understand and evaluate strategies include:

Product Life Cycle (PLC)

This model is used for finding the stage a product has reached in its life cycle. The cycle is in four stages: introduction, growth, maturity and decline. These have been derived from the biological life cycle of birth, growth, maturity, senility and death. It is difficult to gauge the useful life of a product as it is not always possible to predict market demand. Guinness "Light" is an example of a product which failed to take off despite massive R&D and advertising expenditure. At the end of the day the public will decide whether or not they will buy a product. Consequently, some products will not exist for long if they do not catch on. Yet others have an exceptionally long life, for example, the Mini, VW Beetle and the Morris Minor.

The assessment of a product's life cycle is conjecture because human psychology is unpredictable and sales may be boosted by additional sales promotion in the short term. A company should try to have products that sell themselves, as it is essential to avoid excessive sales promotion expenditure on a product that is in decline. Examples of such products include branded chocolates, soap powder, margarine and cereals. Its important for a business to know when to discontinue a product and when to introduce new or modified products.

The replacement of a product should ideally take place just as it has reached its peak, because it can only go into decline after that. If a product which has reached its peak, can be replaced by an equally profitable product then the level of profit can be maintained. Some consumer products have very long life cycles. Examples, to name but a few, include Coca-Cola, Pepsi Cola, Bovril and Persil. The PLC is illustrated below.

Product Life Cycle

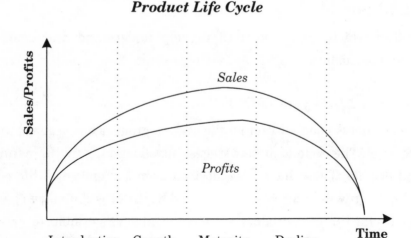

Growth Share or BCG Matrix

The Boston Consulting Group matrix divides products into four categories: stars, cash cows, dogs and question marks or wild cats.

• *Stars* are products or strategic business units which are growing rapidly and need large amounts of cash to maintain their position. They are leaders in their business and also generate large amounts of cash. Cash flows in and out will be roughly in balance and represent the best opportunities for expansion.

• *Cash cows* are low growth, high market share products or divisions. Because of their market share, they have low costs and generate lots of cash. Since growth is slow, reinvestment costs are low. Cash cows provide funds for overheads, dividends, and investment for the rest of the company. They are the foundation on which the company is built.

• *Dogs* are products or divisions with low growth and a low market share and therefore poor profits. They may need cash to survive. The dogs should be minimised by concentration, divestment or liquidation.

• *Question marks* or *wild cats* are high growth, low market share products or divisions. Their conditions are the worst, for their cash needs are high, but cash generation is low. Difficult decisions need to be taken with question marks. They may become stars with the right investment. On the other hand, they could become dogs and lose you money. These, if left in the cell become "cash traps". Since growth is high, market share should be easier to get for them than for dogs.

Managers need to categorise their products and business units into the four types of the Growth Share Matrix. Hard decisions may then need to be taken to optimise the profitability of the business. The BCG Matrix is shown below.

Growth Share Matrix

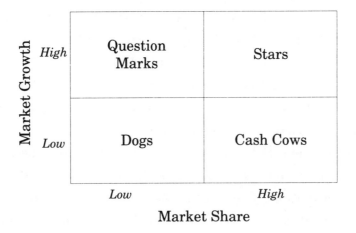

The Profit Impact of Market Strategy (PIMS)

PIMS is a practical model that relates a wide range of strategic and situational variables to profitability and cash flow. The strategic variables include market share, product quality, and vertical integration. The situational variables include market growth rate, industry stage of development, and capital intensity. In simple terms, its purpose is to determine what strategies work best under what market conditions. It suggests that large market share equals large profits. It is based on an analysis of over 1,000 businesses of more than 150 large and small companies. Some of their findings suggest that a broad line of products is more profitable, early in the life cycle. However, a broad product line is more important in capital-intensive industry. Contrary to the findings of PIMS, niche products and services can be highly profitable for organisations.

Diffusion Analysis

The way a new product is taken up by society. Initially, new products are taken up by a small number of pioneering customers, known as innovators, which account for about 2.5 per cent of the population. These are followed by sophisticated people, known as early adopters, who form about 13.5 per cent of the population. These are in turn followed by conservative (but above average status) people, known as the early majority, and they form about 34 per cent of the population. Next come the people of below average status, known as the late majority, which also form about 34 per cent of the population. Lastly, come the low status people, known as laggards, who view life through the rear-view mirror. These form about 16 per cent of the population. This is a very useful model which may help you predict sales of a new product or service over its expected lifetime. Eventually, the product may become a mass market item with widespread demand. The Diffusion of Innovation Curve is shown below.

Diffusion of Innovation Curve

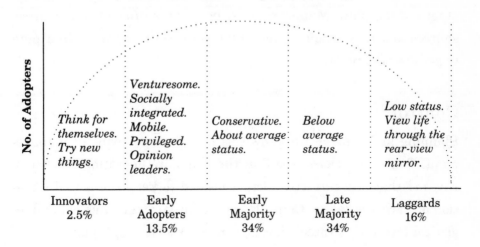

Discounted Cash Flow (DCF)

Capital investment appraisal methods such as payback, accounting rate of return, internal rate of return and net present value, can be used to evaluate the financial viability of developing new products or entry into new markets. DCF is very useful for giving you the likely bottom-line result taking into account cash inflows and out-flows and the time value of money, for a particular investment.

Implementation

The strategic plan is management's blueprint for what they intend to do. Strategies are just pie in the sky if they are not implemented through operational plans, action programmes, policies, budgets, organisation structures, systems and procedures. The structure and resources must be provided to support the implementation of strategies. Everybody involved must know what is required of them and should be committed to the successful implementation of the strategic plan. Senior management must be held accountable for the success or failure of the plan. Strong leadership from the top is needed to push the plan through and to motivate staff to get the work done. Sub-goals and targets will need to be in place to monitor stages of the plan. Managers must be given sufficient financial resources to achieve their targets. Plan your work and work your plan to get the best results.

Control

Planning and control are known as the Siamese twins of management. Control checks to see that the plans are operating satisfactorily and that any corrective action needed to keep the actual situation on target is taken. Controls operate at strategic, tactical and logistical levels: at strategic levels, through the strategic plans; at tactical level, through the annual business plans, production and marketing plans, and budgets including capital and revenue budgets; at logistical level, through sales targets, cash budgets, weekly production plans, daily schedules and management-by-objectives schemes. The characteristics of good control can be recalled by the mnemonic ACTRESS:

- **A**ction-orientated. They should trigger off the appropriate corrective action.

- **C**onsistent, complete and comprehensive. The control information should be reliable and consistent from period to period.

- **T**imely. In a business, out-of-date information is water under the bridge and of limited or no value. Hence the need for monthly accounts.

- **R**elevant. The information should be relevant to the person receiving it. For example, a supervisor should get operational-type information while a director should get strategic information. Balance sheets would be of little value to a supervisor, while stockout rates might not be of interest to a director.

- **E**conomic. It should be economical to produce and the benefits achieved by its production should exceed the cost of producing the information. Producing information is costly and so it should serve a real purpose.

- **Simple.** Remember the KISS technique. Keep it simple, stupid! It should be user-friendly, in that the people who receive it will have no problem understanding it.

- **Significant.** MBE (management by exception). Information should be prioritised so that only important issues receive attention.

Advantages of Strategic Planning

- Develops a mission and corporate objectives and audits its present resources.

- Systematically considers the strengths and weaknesses of a company in relation to its competitors. It aims to exploit strengths and minimise or eliminate weaknesses.

- Reduces risk because the threats and opportunities are systematically reviewed.

- Encourages creativity and initiative by considering possible alternatives.

- Decision making should be improved because the purpose is clearly defined and the means to achieve that purpose clearly spelt out.

- Charts future change through the environmental analysis and means of dealing with that change.

- It give a sense of purpose to staff. Ideally, staff should be involved in the process and the plan should be made known to them.

- Plans are formalised and systematic which means nothing is overlooked and alternatives are considered.

The CHOICE Model

The CHOICE model covers the various types of thinking involved in strategic planning. Different types of thinking are required for different stages of the SPEWSIC model. CHOICE is a memory jogger for:

- **Critical.** Critical thinking exercises your critical judgement. It is logical and analytical. It is the kind of thinking that prevents us from making stupid mistakes. The position audit and environmental analysis are examples of this type of thinking in strategic planning.

- **Having control.** This is the type of thinking involved in organising, planning and controlling. Corporate objectives, sales targets, critical path analyses, Gantt charts, variance analysis, budgets and benchmarks help us to exercise control by comparing actual performance against agreed standards. The control stage of the SPEWSIC model is governed by this type of thinking.

- **Optimism.** This is the positive point of view. A vision statement is usually framed in optimistic terms. Without pursuing the seemingly impossible we would never progress. In SWOT analysis it will emphasise the strengths and opportunities while playing down the weaknesses and threats.

- **Information.** This thinking looks for quantitative and fact-based information. Sales forecasts, projected profit and loss accounts and balance sheets often underscore strategic plans. It is the type of thinking that accountants excel in. Because of the ubiquitous computer and its great ability to produce information quickly there is a temptation to rely too much on this type of thinking and to neglect our intuitive powers.

- **Creative.** This is the type of thinking needed to generate options and strategies which the business might consider. Well-known business strategies can be combined in new and novel ways to give you creative ideas for the future. Developing new products and services and new markets for existing products would be examples of this type of thinking.

- **Emotional.** This is concerned with feelings, intuition and emotions. This type of thinking resides in the subconscious. It is holistic, synthesizing and integrating and will often produce the flashes of brilliance that go on to be huge business success stories. Many successful businesses were the result of intuition rather than information and critical judgement. For example, inventor Art Fry of 3M was a singer in a choir. His bookmarks kept on falling out of his hymnbook. From this he got the idea for Post-it notes. This little yellow sticker is now an essential item of office stationery. Nevertheless, intuitive thinking needs to be tempered by the other types of thinking for best results. The Post-it note required considerable research and development expenditure and marketing before it became the commercial success story it is today. Intuition must be followed and supported by critical, control and information-type thinking.

Edwin Land was the inventor of non-glare Polaroid glass, instant film and the instant camera. He maintained that every significant step in every field is achieved by people who think in an intuitive and unconventional way. Their friends and colleagues may be more intelligent and better educated but they have not mastered the art of looking at things from a fresh perspective. Many people thought the railway was a stupid idea — some farmers believed that the noise of the train would prevent hens from laying eggs.

People ridiculed Robert Fulton's steamboat as "Fulton's Folly". All progress has initially been derided and opposed. The printing press, telegraph, telephone, electric light and typewriter were all greeted with hostility when initially suggested. However, hostility and disbelieve didn't deter the Wright brothers, Orville and Wilbur who flew the first successful aeroplane in 1903.

Summary

The ability to think strategically is important if you want to be successful in your personal and professional life. The helicopter viewpoint is the ability to see the big picture. The eight Ps of success for business management are:

- Purpose

- Plan

- Passion

- Principle

- Product

- Position

- Profit

- People.

The SPEWSIC is a very useful model to help you think in a strategic mode. This stands for:

- Strategic objectives

- Position audit

- Environmental analysis

- Wots up analysis

- Strategies to fill the gap

- Implementation

- Control.

It might be worthwhile committing this mnemonic to memory.

Some common business strategies were discussed such as:

- Organic growth

- Growth by acquisition

- Marketing mix

- Strategic alliances

- Joint ventures

- Franchising

- Leasing

- Licensing

- Mergers

- Divestment

- Management buyouts

- Corporate venturing.

Well-known strategic business models were discussed:

- Product Life Cycle (PLC)

- Growth Share Matrix or the Boston Consulting Group Matrix (BCG)

- Profit Impact of Marketing Strategy (PIMS)

- Diffusion of innovation curve

- Discounted Cash Flow (DCF).

The CHOICE thinking model was discussed. This memory jogger stands for:

- Critical

- Have control

- Optimism

- Information

- Creative

- Emotional

Different types of thinking are required for different stages of the SPEWSIC model.

Chapter 3 Mind Map

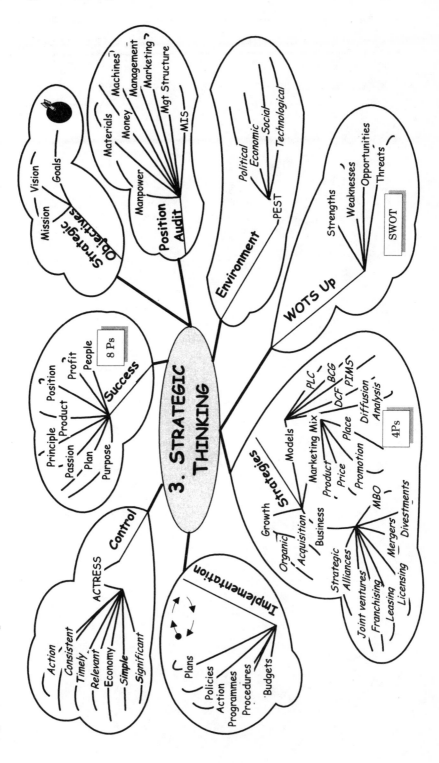

4. Communication

"To effectively communicate, we must realize that we are all different in the way we perceive the world and use this understanding as a guide to our communication with others." — Anthony Robbins

---

♦ *What are the PICTURE & GRAPEVINE models?*

♦ *How do perceptions affect communication?*

♦ *How can you manage conflict?*

♦ *What are the various types of questions?*

♦ *How can you use language effectively?*

♦ *How can you negotiate effectively?*

♦ *What are the basic skills for running meetings?*

♦ *What are the various types of interview?*

The Importance of Communication

It is an understatement to say that communication is one of the key skills of successful managers. Managers spend most of their lives communicating in one way or another. They need to know the most effective ways of getting their point across. Apart from normal social intercourse a manager will spend a considerable amount of time attending meetings, interviewing, negotiating, mentoring, counselling and coaching. From time to time most managers will need to know how to manage conflict and how to handle the unpleasant task of disciplining an employee.

The PICTURE Model

This stands for:

- **Pitch.** This is the degree of highness or lowness in your voice. You should vary your pitch in relation to your needs for emphasis or otherwise. Observe and model the way that news presenters do it on television. As a general rule use a high pitch to communicate excitement. Use a low pitch to communicate control. Move your voice up at the end of a question. Change to higher or lower notes to add emphasis within a particular sentence. Use the same pitch throughout if you want to bore your audience to tears. Nothing irritates more than a high pitched or squeaky voice.

- **Inflexion** is similar to pitch and includes how you modulate your voice. For example, you may raise or lower your voice at the end of a sentence or just before certain words for effect.

- **Courtesy.** Observe the normal courtesies. "Please" and "Thank you" should be a normal part of your vocabulary. Use the person's name frequently during the conversation. Maintain an appropriate level of eye contact and match body language. Demonstrating courtesy, concern, respect, acceptance, support, openness, and honesty is critical to successful communication.

- **Tone.** Become aware of your tone. Tone can be friendly, indifferent, angry or even rude. You need to develop a pleasant and friendly tone of voice. Tone is particularly noticeable on the phone. People with melodic voices are perceived to have a socially attractive personality. We assume that they are nice and kind.

- **U**nderstanding. Avoid arrogance. Don't interrupt. Seek first to understand.

- **R**ate. A slow rate of speech can be used to emphasise the importance or seriousness of material. A faster rate can be used for less serious topics. The average rate of speech is 125 words per minute. We think at about four times that rate. Vary your rate of speech to hold the interest of your listener and prevent mind drift. People who talk faster than average are perceived by many as above average intelligence.

- **E**nunciation. Pronounce your words carefully. Be clear and distinct to get your message across. You are judged to a large extent by the way that you speak. Slurring words, mispronouncing words or speaking with an accent that people find difficult to understand will all detract from your communication. People may make judgements regarding your education and social class by the way that you speak. Always avoid the use of bad language or slang. People with middle-class accents are sometimes perceived to be more competent and intelligent.

The GRAPEVINE Model

This stands for:

- **G**esture. Use your body language to effect. The hands can reinforce or detract from points made. Study some of the great modern speakers. They are as accessible as your nearest TV. Model yourself on them. President Clinton is a superb speaker and is worthy of imitation. The well-known SLANT model method suggests that you should: **S**it up; **L**ean forward; **A**sk questions; **N**od your head and **T**alk as appropriate.

- **R**ecurring pauses. Pausing for a few seconds here and there can be quite effective and gives emphasis to points made. To you a few seconds will seem like ages but the audience will hardly notice. A pause placed immediately before a main idea or the climax of a story can create suspense. A pause placed immediately after a key idea can add emphasis. However, prolonged silence can be a source of embarrassment.

- **Appearance.** Dress your best. People do notice and certainly you will be judged to a certain extent by your appearance.

- **Posture.** Stand erect to project confidence and lean forward occasionally to show involvement and interest. Sloppy posture creates a very bad impression and may indicate pomposity, lack of interest or unconcern.

- **Eye contact.** Study for eye accessing cues and match as appropriate. Maintain eye contact, but don't stare. When speaking to a group, span your eye contact across the group and don't linger too long on any one individual.

- **Voice.** Should be clear and at the appropriate level. Study the PICTURE model above.

- **Involving the listener.** Be open to new views, ideas and paradigms. Lean towards the listener to show interest and concern. Listen twice as much as you speak. Harvey Jackins, the founder of co-counselling, once remarked: "Everybody, the whole world over, just wants to be listened to; the trouble is, so does everyone else."

- **Natural self.** Be your natural self. Pretending to be something you aren't is not going to impress and will actually irritate your audience.

- **Entertaining.** Smile and use humour as appropriate. Of all the things you wear, your expression is the most important. The situation will dictate whether or not humour is suitable. Avoid sexist or cultural jokes, however, as they can offend.

Perception

Our communication is influenced by perception which in turn affects the way we see, react to, rationalise away and interpret events. Objective reality and our perception of it is not necessarily the same. The map is not the territory. This is because perception is not passive. It is active and we construct, interpret, and influence what we see. We process all information through the senses of seeing, hearing and feeling. Our perception of events is influenced by selecting one aspect to see and ignoring others, our past experiences, our personality and our current needs. Our values, beliefs, attitudes, moods and interests also influence what we notice, what we pay attention to and what we ignore. You see what you believe. Beliefs act as self-fulfilling prophecies.

Halo Effect

When you like or respect a person you are normally going to be very well disposed towards them. Some of the older generation, despite the overwhelming evidence, are incapable of believing that members of the clergy perpetrated sexual abuse. In standard psychological tests, if the person doing the testing likes the person being tested they are likely to give them higher scores than otherwise. Another tester might give different scores. In an interview situation a manager might see a person as honest and enthusiastic and also mark them up on traits such as loyalty, courtesy and efficiency even though there is no link between the first set of traits and the second. The *horn effect* is the opposite of the halo effect where a manager dislikes a person and marks them down accordingly.

Values

Values are things we hold dear or believe to be intrinsically desirable. Sometimes we assume that our values are the same as somebody else's. As a manager we may assume that all staff desire promotion. However, some people do not desire promotion because of the responsibility or disruption involved. Therefore, a manager's attempts to use promotion as a motivational carrot can often prove to be counterproductive. Some companies claim values such as honesty, equality, participation, excellence, quality, customer satisfaction and so on. However, if they fail to "walk the talk" such values will mean nothing.

Perceptual Readiness

We see what we expect to see because our values and beliefs predispose us to interpret what we see in a certain way. Managers should be aware that if they have high expectations for their staff and treat them like adults the staff are likely to live up to their high expectations. On the other hand, if they treat them like children they are likely to behave in an immature way. This is the reason why staff may oppose or actively obstruct any little workplace change and even on occasions threaten or take part in industrial action.

Attribution Theory

People usually attribute others' behaviour to their personality or to their situation. A manager, for example, may wonder whether a worker's hostility reflects an aggressive personality or whether the worker is stressed because of poor working conditions. In practice, we tend to underestimate situational causes of behaviour and over-estimate personality causes. For example, a manager may believe that a worker's poor timekeeping is due to personality defects such as lack of responsibility, consideration or commitment. In fact, the poor timekeeping may be caused by a domestic situation — the worker's wife is sick and he has the task of getting his children to school. This cause is likely to be overlooked unless the manager has the wisdom to make subtle background enquiries.

In relation to ourselves, on the other hand, we tend to adopt the opposite point of view when explaining our own behaviour. We tend to emphasise the situation rather than the personality. Thus any stress experienced is caused by tight deadlines rather than personality defects.

Self-serving bias is another form of attribution. People are inclined to present themselves in a favourable light. They attribute their success to their own abilities and efforts rather than to being in the right place at the right time.

To be effective in their jobs managers need to understand how their perceptions of their own and others' behaviours are influenced by personality or situational factors.

Perceptual Defence

We tend to avoid hearing and seeing unpleasant things. People have blind spots in their beliefs and tend to hear only nice things said about them and to block out unpleasant things. Not taking the tip from your manager about doing something about undesirable aspects of your job performance may cost you the next promotion! So listen for the bad things as well as the good. Self-development is about accepting feedback and taking corrective action to eliminate undesirable behaviours.

Stereotyping

Stereotypes are collections of prejudices. If they are not discriminatory or negatively used they can be a useful way of understanding people. We may consider all Americans loud, all Scotsmen mean, and all Italians to be temperamental. However, like any category scheme they can be dangerous and blind us to individual differences. As a manager we should be aware of how we label people. Our view of people may be based as much on our own biases and prejudices as on the person's actual behaviour and personality. Our judgement about a person may say as much about ourselves as the other person.

Cognitive Dissonance

This is the internal conflict and anxiety that people experience when they encounter information at variance with their values. People do not feel comfortable with dissonance. As a result they try to remove or reduce it. They may try to get new information, change their interpretation of events, reverse their decision, or change their values. They may even refuse to believe the dissonant input, or rationalise it out of the way. In a well-known study, adults who were paid a lot of money to tell a lie rationalised lying simply by telling themselves that the amount of money justified just one lie. People offered less money managed to convince themselves they weren't really lying at all — the bribe was worthless so the lie didn't matter. In a recent court case reported in the newspapers a priest rationalised away sexual abuse of children saying it was merely a venal sin and as such did not conflict with his vows of celibacy and chastity. Recently a politician accused of bribery and corruption rationalised it away as begrudgery. It seem that people can justify any wrongdoing in their own minds.

Group Think

This is the tendency for like-minded people within a cohesive group to agree on issues without challenging each other's ideas rationally or analysing problems logically. The problem may arise in groups such as a board of directors with a strong charismatic leader. Handy notes that "ultra-cohesive groups can be dangerous because in the organisational context the group must serve the organisa- tion, not itself". Hence institutions, contrary to declared values, show more concern to protect their corrupt members than to serve the interests of their customers. Groups can start pursuing their own ends rather than the interests of the organisation. The group- think process can be checked by appointing a "devil's advocate" whose role is to challenge ideas, question facts and logic, and provide constructive criticism. The symptoms of group think can be recalled by the mnemonic STORMING:

- **S**elf-censorship. Members of the group want to maintain consensus and so put pressure on dissidents not to "rock the boat". The "club" mentality prevails.

- **T**endency to stereotype. This is the perception of others as outsiders and opponents and to vilify them as the "enemy" — a "them and us" perception. For example, competitors may be seen as evil, weak and incompetent.

- **O**ppression to prevent dissent. There is strong group pressure put on members who disagree to prevent them from dissenting.

- **R**ationalisation. Inconsistent facts are rationalised away to quash doubt or remorse.

- **M**oral blindness. This is a belief in the supreme morality of the group — "might is right."

- **I**nvulnerability. The group is very optimistic and is willing to take undue risks in the belief that the group is invulnerable. They are blind to the risks and dangers involved in their "pet" strategies.

- **N**ullify divergent views. There is an erroneous perception of unanimity and divergent views are filtered out and ignored.

- **G**uard the decision by mutual support. The solidarity of the group is maintained at all costs.

Irving Janis, the psychologist who identified the phenomenon of groupthink, gives several historical examples of groupthink:

- The decision to launch the Bay of Pigs invasion of Cuba

- The decision not to fly reconnaissance mission north of Hawaii just before the Japanese attack on Pearl Harbour.

- The decision to invade North Korea

- The decision to bomb North Vietnam.

Interpersonal Conflict

Interpersonal conflict is a major reason for the breakdown in communications in an organisation. The sources of interpersonal conflict can be recalled by the mnemonic TRIPE:

- **T**erritorial instinct. People are social animals and the territorial instinct is just as strong in people as it is in other animals. Departments have their own areas of responsibility; people have their own jobs, offices, chairs or parking spaces. All of these may give rise to resentment, jealousy and conflict. Strangers walking in to another person's office can cause suspicion and upset. People sitting in another's usual spot can cause offence. Departments mistakenly doing another's work may cause an interdepartmental dispute. Staff inadvertently doing another's duties may cause a demarcation dispute.

- **R**ole incompatibility. Some roles in organisations are naturally incompatible with others because of different goals and priorities. For example, accountants try to cut costs by minimising the investment in working capital, while marketing people wish to have stock at all times to meet the needs of customers. Production people favour long production runs for reasons of economy while sales people prefer variety of products which require short production runs to meet customer demands. The resulting conflict may have to be resolved by the chief executive.

- **I**nformation deficiency. People from different departments have different professional training and specialisation. They speak different technical languages which can cause misunderstanding and confusion. For example, accountants usually have problems trying to communicate financial issues to other managers. Information technology is rife with jargon. All of this hinders communication. However, these differences are not emotionally charged and can be resolved with proper training in communication skills.

- **Personal.** Personal differences arise because of age, gender, experience, education, religion, specialisation, values, beliefs, attitude, culture and class. These differences can often become emotionally charged with moral overtones. They are the usual reasons for personality clashes.

- **Environmental stress.** Business process re-engineering with possibilities of restructuring, redundancy and retraining can cause uncertainty, stress and ultimately conflict. In more normal times competition for scarce budgetary resources can cause interdepartmental conflict.

Organisational Conflict

Some problems in organisations are hidden while others are more obvious. The organisational iceberg model is a useful way of understanding the visible and hidden aspects of organisational problems. This model is shown on the following page. According to this model the overt parts of an organisation are visible such as the formal organisation structure. This includes job descriptions, levels of management, spans of control, corporate objectives, strategic plans, business plans and policies and procedures. Concentrating on these will only give you a partial view of a complex social system.

To get a total view of organisational problems you need to examine the covert parts of an organisation as well. The covert parts include the social and psychological aspects of the way people interact, think, feel and behave. This includes group norms, organisational politics, interpersonal relationships, interdepartmental conflicts, rivalry for budgetary resources, values, beliefs, attitudes and corporate culture. By taking into account both the overt and covert aspects of organisational life a better perspective is obtained and more informed decisions will be made. In many conflict situations the overt aspects of the problem are only symptomatic of real underlying causes. Unless these underlying causes are tackled the problem will not be solved. Many problems are caused by distrust of management and poor communication.

Iceberg Model

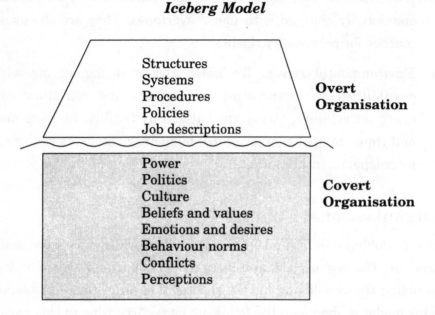

Structures
Systems
Procedures
Policies
Job descriptions

Overt Organisation

Power
Politics
Culture
Beliefs and values
Emotions and desires
Behaviour norms
Conflicts
Perceptions

Covert Organisation

Resolving Conflict

There are some simple rules of thumb which will help a manager handle conflict:

- Look, listen and learn. Identify the source of conflict and learn from past mistakes. The TRIPE model will help you categorise the source of the conflict and therefore the type of policies and strategies necessary for resolution. Build in a cooling off period into the resolution phase. Reason will not prevail when nerves are frayed and tempers are high.

- As a manager you should model the type of behaviour you expect others to adopt. An open communication style and a participative approach to management encourages trust, collaboration and conflict resolution.

- Stick to the facts; don't personalise or emotionalise issues. Deal with sources of conflict quickly and resolutely.

- Aim for win-win solutions. This way everybody comes out of the situation feeling positive and reasonably happy.

- Train employees in interpersonal relationship skills, communication skills, problem solving, team building and conflict resolution.

- Good personnel policies and procedures in areas like grievances, discipline, arbitration and conciliation will eliminate possible sources of conflict.

- Fair and imaginative distribution of budgetary resources will reduce a possible source of conflict.

- Improve job satisfaction through empowerment, job restructuring and reward systems.

Conflict Styles

The conflict grid is a useful model for categorising and discussing the various conflict styles. In a work situation you are confronted with two challenges:

- Getting the job done within budgetary and time constraints, and

- Getting along with other people.

In the conflict grid the vertical axis is concerned with interpersonal relations or getting along with other people. The horizontal axis is concerned with getting the job done. Obviously a balance between the two skills should be your objective. The grid is shown below.

- *Competing*. A competing style is a high concern for getting the job done and a low concern for interpersonal relationships. The focus is on the task and the need to get along with other people is forgotten about. This style may provoke anger, resentment, hostility, confrontation and aggressiveness.

- *Accommodating*. This style is a high concern for getting along with people and a low concern for getting the job done. It is known as accommodating because the person using this style will accommodate the other person's wishes at all costs. The person with this style tends to be unassertive, co-operative, submissive and obliging. The objective is to avoid hurting the other person's feelings if at all possible.

The Conflict Grid

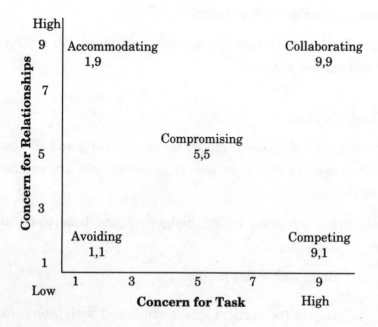

Source: Blake and Mouton (1964).

- *Avoiding*. This style is a low concern for both relationships and for getting the task done. A person with this style is indifferent to outcomes. They are in complete denial that a conflict situation exists. They adopt an ostrich-like approach with their heads buried in the sand. They believe that if they ignore the situation it will go away.

- *Compromising*. This person has moderate concern for getting the job done and getting along with other people. Tactics of compromise include uncertainty, conciliation and concessions. This is a lose-lose situation leaving both parties dissatisfied.

- *Collaborating*. This is a high concern for people and a high concern for getting the job done. This style values co-operation, joint problem solving and the achievement of goals. This is a win-win situation with both parties satisfied.

The Power of Language

If poorly understood, language can limit our communication and achievements in life. We are a product of our thoughts. They really do influence and determine our actions. Language is the doorway to our perceptual maps. Language helps us understand our own map of reality and the other person's map of reality. You can decide to communicate in a general or in a specific way. Each strategy has its uses. For example, when addressing a large diverse group you can talk in a general way and let each person interpret what you say in line with their own experiences. When talking to a smaller group from a similar background you can talk more specifically by addressing their specific concerns. In fact, you can change your strategy by becoming general or specific as the need arises. Whatever strategy you adopt, choose your words with care.

We will now consider some well-known ideas about the power of language to limit or enhance our abilities. Know your own thinking and language preferences and notice how others express their thoughts. The following are some common problems with the use of language. Keep these in mind when interpreting communication. They may alert you to the need to probe further to question assumptions.

Deletions

We are selective about the way we describe our experiences. We leave things out. In other words we delete them. Either they do not register or we discount them as not important. In a simple deletion, information is simply missing from a statement. For example, you might hear the expression: "He is angry." The question that should be asked is: "Angry about what, or whom?" You obviously need more information.

Another kind of deletion is called comparative deletions. You might have heard someone making an observation: "He is a talented person." The question which should be asked is: "More talented than whom?" Benchmarks or standards for comparison will make the observation more meaningful.

Other statements may lack a reference. "Wouldn't you think they'd do something about it?" Who specifically are "they" and what specifically should they "do" about it? What specifically do we mean by "it"? For example, people usually blame the government for everything: "Why don't they do something?"— "they" inevitably being the government.

Unspecified Verbs and Nouns

Some verbs are very vague, for instance, saying: "He let me down." There is a lot of missing information here that is crucial to the real meaning. "How exactly did he let you down?" Sometimes people are vague on purpose. You have to recognise the situation and decide whether or not you need to probe further. Unspecified nouns can have different meanings depending on how the person uses the words. For example: "I need a break." "What sort of a break do you need — a ten-minute break, a short holiday or an extended holiday?" "Why do you need a break?" "What do you need a break from?" "Where do you need to go on the break?"

Distortions

We distort things to match our views, values and beliefs. We exaggerate or diminish experience to suit our own inclinations. We presuppose things which, when we examine them closely, are not really valid. For example, you may have heard: "You can't teach an old dog new tricks" and "You can't make a silk purse out of a sow's ear." The validity of such statements can obviously be questioned. "What is stopping you from learning at your age?" People who go back to college later in life actually do better than their younger colleagues. Two research chemists treated sow's ears chemically and extracted a silk filament which they made into a silk purse.

Mind-reading

We mind-read all the time. This is where we assume knowledge of another which you couldn't possibly have unless you were able to jump inside their mind. A common example would be: "You don't like me." "How do you know that I don't like you?" "What leads you to believe that?" We attribute views to other people all the time without checking out the facts.

Cause and Effect

We are taught from early childhood that actions have consequences. This is known as the law of cause and effect. For example, you may have concluded that the boss makes you nervous. However, if you think about this you begin to see how erroneous it is. This is in fact an unsupported conclusion. Nobody can make you nervous, only yourself. It is the thoughts in your mind and your imagination which make you nervous, the interpretation you put on these thoughts and how you react to them. Of course, you can control your own thoughts and whether or not you view a particular situation as being a source of nervousness. You may not always be able to control events but you can control your own thoughts.

Generalisations

This is where we take on specific experience to represent a whole class of experiences and ignore exceptions. It is useful because it helps us make sense of the world about us. It's a problem if we generalise incorrectly or fail to learn from new experiences. Values and beliefs are examples of generalisations. Words like *all, no one, always, never* or *every* are common generalisations. For example, many people say that they have never smoked in their lives. Never? On mature recollection they usually find that they made a few unsuccessful attempts to smoke as children but found it a very unpleasant experience and luckily never pursued the habit. Another common observation is: "All politicians are dishonest." All? On reflection you realise that this statement is untrue because you know that the vast majority of politicians are in fact honest.

Words of Possibility

These are words which suggest things that we can or cannot do. They fuel self-limiting beliefs. They imply that we have no choice. They often include negative words like *can't, haven't* or *won't*. A common example might be: "I can't concentrate." A response might be: "What is stopping you from concentrating?" On reflection you find its a matter of dedication, motivation and practice. Take the "T" out of can't and change your life! Think instead of what can be done and what is possible.

Words of Necessity

These words imply that we must do something. Common examples are words like *must, must not, ought, ought not, have to, should* and *shouldn't*. "I must do this." "I mustn't do that." In reality, there is only "one must" in life and that is we must all die sooner or later. These words have been inputted into our minds in childhood by parents and authority figures. Subconsciously they prevent us from taking actions which may in fact be in our own interest. The response should be: "What would happen if you didn't?" Such language is very common which shows that many of our attitudes, values and beliefs go unquestioned.

Questions — The FLOOR Technique

Questions can be formulated to encourage or discourage discussion. The FLOOR mnemonic covers some of the most important types of questions which you can use:

- **F**actual questions. This type of question seeks facts, information, data and so on. "How many of you have attended a strategic planning course?" This question will elicit a fact-based response.

- **L**eading questions. This type of question tries to direct and control the discussion. "This problem is impossible to solve, isn't it?" Leading questions discourage discussion and debate. These type of questions are often used by lawyers to trap their adversaries and support their case. Leading questions are inappropriate where you want to explore issues, encourage discussion and debate.

- **O**pen questions. This type of question is expressed in very broad terms in order to facilitate open communication. Such a question is capable of a wide range of answers. It is usually prefaced by who, what, when, where, how and why. "How can we evaluate training?" Open questions are ideal for opening up issues, exploring alternatives, brainstorming and for problem-solving situations.

- **Overhead questions.** These are questions which are addressed to the group as a whole. You may wish to stimulate thinking for all participants in the group. Putting the question to the group as a whole encourages participants to reflect on the issue. On the other hand, asking direct questions only engages specific individuals and may lose the interest and attention of others. It can be used to draw out the experience of a quiet participant but should be used with care in order not to embarrass. It can also be used to break up private conversations at a meeting or to interrupt a talkative participant by asking the views of someone else.

- **Redirected questions.** This is where the group leader redirects a question to the other members of the group. This keeps the group actively involved. Also, in a situation where you don't know the answer yourself, it may be a cute way of getting off the hook! Another type of question is the rhetorical question. In the case of a rhetorical question the leader does not expect the group to answer and the group knows this. "What else could I do but follow the majority decision?" This type of question has no value in discussion leading but may provoke thought.

Basic Negotiation Skills

Most of us spend a lot of time negotiating even if we don't realise it. You negotiate with customers, suppliers, the boss, staff, colleagues and with your children and partner on a daily basis. Examples include getting the best deal on a trade-in against a new car, negotiating a pay rise for yourself or selecting a builder to build an extension to your home. Therefore, basic negotiation skills can prove to be very useful in everyday life as well as in business.

A sound approach to negotiation can be recalled by the mnemonic POCKET:

- **P**lanning. Just like any endeavour planning and preparation are the key to success in negotiations. Do your homework. This takes time but will pay dividends when it comes to the bargaining stage. Set clear objectives for yourself. You should have a clear view of the outcomes you desire. Now consider the strategy you will adopt to achieve your objectives. Consider the other party's needs, priorities and perspectives. The key to planning a successful win-win negotiation is to constantly put yourself in the other party's shoes. Consider where the meeting will be held and the seating arrangements. A neutral venue is probably the best as the home advantage is avoided. If the negotiations are going to be done on a team basis, pick the best people for your team. People with past experience as successful negotiators will be an obvious choice.

- **O**pening position. Consider what your opening position is. Consider what the other party's opening position is likely to be. Consider your cut-off point or the minimum that you would accept and the likely cut-off point of the other party. Consider what needs to be done to bring the two positions nearer the middle. Think in terms of desirable ranges rather than absolutes. Aim for a win-win outcome rather than a win-lose outcome. A win-win outcome satisfies both parties. A win-lose outcome only creates resentment which may return to haunt you in the future. Before you begin make sure that the other party has the required authority to conclude an agreement. Open the discussion on a neutral subject such as the weather in order to build rapport. Exercise all your diplomacy skills.

- **C**ommunicating. The normal rules of communication apply. Using clear words, appropriate body language and listening effectively are needed. Ask a lot of questions so that you identify the other party's wants and needs. Use the technique of reflective listening such as "you feel that . . ." This will help you avoid confrontation while at the same time giving you an opportunity to find out how the other party thinks. Practise your best interpersonal relationship skills. Avoid emotive language and insults. Always maintain your composure. The problem for negotiation should be clearly identified. If it is a major one it should be broken down into smaller parts for resolution. This will facilitate agreement as parts which have been agreed can be outlined and put aside and parts awaiting agreement can be isolated for further negotiation. However, keep your eye on the long-term objective. During the course of negotiation the other person's position should be summarised now and again so that both parties know where they stand.

- **K**now your opponent. What are the other party's objectives? What will they settle for? Visualise what it would feel like to be your opponent and try to see things from their viewpoint. Identify the tradables you can bargain with and assess how valuable they are to you and to the other party. Rank each tradable as to priority, high, medium and low from your perspective and also from the other party's perspective. Bargaining is all about trading concessions. You offer something in order to get something in return. The key point about concessions is to never give anything away without getting something in return. Benjamin Franklin said: "Trades would not take place unless it were advantageous to the parties concerned. Of course, it is better to strike as good a bargain as one's bargaining position admits. The worst outcome is when by overriding greed, no bargain is struck, and a trade that could have been advantageous to both parties, does not come off at all."

- **E**xplore options. Use "what if?" questions to find out what the other party would settle for. The more options considered the more likely that a win-win solution will result. This is part of the process of searching for common ground and coming up with a workable compromise. Win-win solutions are arrived at through asking questions, creativity and problem solving. They require openness, imagination, trust and goodwill.

- **Terminate.** Agreement is reached when an option which satisfies both parties is selected. It is important that everything agreed is put in writing to avoid misunderstandings in the future. Copies of the agreement should be circulated to all relevant parties.

Negotiation Strategies

The various negotiation strategies can be recalled by the mnemonic SLAPDASH:

- **Salami.** This is chunking down your objectives into sub-objectives and achieving a sub-objective at a time. It is a divide-and-conquer approach. Little by little you may achieve your objective. Achieving a sub-goal gives you a feeling of accomplishment and motivates you forward to achieve more sub-goals and so on. As a sub-goal is achieved it can be put aside and the next one concentrated on. Start with the items where there is little disagreement.

- **Limited authority.** As a sham you claim that anything else other than what's on the table would require approval by a higher authority. It is thus outside your control. This is a risky strategy as it may end the negotiations. However, it does give the other party an opportunity to review their position. The strategy may also backfire in that the other party may call the bluff and insist that they go to the higher authority.

- **Apparent withdrawal.** This is a bit of deception and pretence on the part of one party. They withdraw from negotiation because they claim that a reasonable offer has not been made. They hope that the other party will have a change of heart and come back with a better offer. The success of the sham depends on one's acting ability.

- **Pretence.** This might be flying a kite to test the waters. It's the principle of "you don't know how deep the puddle is until you step in it". Unions usually come in with a very high figure partly to see what reaction they'll get from the employer. Politicians do it all the time. They leak some "confidential information" about a proposed new policy to see what the public reaction is likely to be. If the reaction is favourable they will then pursue the strategy. If the reaction is unfavourable they will quietly drop it.

- **Deadlines.** Time deadlines may be imposed to concentrate minds and energies. It's surprising what can be achieved when people are working to tight schedules. If the other party has set the deadline you can always test it to see if it can be changed. The Belfast Agreement is an example where this strategy seems to have worked. The parties to the agreement were operating to a deadline set by the British Government which was not negotiable.

- **Acting good guy/bad guy.** Popularised in films and television serials, this is the strategy used by police to break down the resistance of the bad guy. One member of a negotiating team may take a hard-line aggressive approach while another adopts a more friendly and reasonable stance. When the bad guy leaves the room, the good guy offers a deal which in the circumstances looks comparatively attractive.

- **Standard practice.** One party tries to convince another that the contract on offer is standard in the business and acceptable to all. An employer may make a pay offer claiming it's what has been accepted in the industry generally. However, if you challenge the contract or offer you'll often be surprised by the favourable results that can be achieved. Details of the standard contract can usually be changed to accommodate your wishes.

- **Hand a *fait accompli*.** An example of this is where you give your car to a garage for an estimate with an instruction to wait for your permission before proceeding with the repairs. However, when you go to the garage you find that the repair has already been carried out without your consent. Most people to avoid hassle will pay up although you could refuse payment and take legal action. Builders have been known to demolish buildings on which there is a preservation order. This is a risky strategy and can go very wrong if the local authorities insist on the building being reinstated!

Meetings

Meetings can be one of the greatest time wasters in management. In addition, they cost a lot of money. There is the cost of the time of all the participants plus any other costs involved such as equipment and stationery. There is also the opportunity cost involved in attending meetings — the other activities which participants could be doing if they didn't have to attend the meeting. Meetings range from the very formal type such as the annual general meeting of a company to briefings between managers and staff and team meetings. Most meetings will need a chairman to lead the meeting and a secretary to look after the minutes and general administration. The same general approach can be used for the organisation of any of these meetings.

Before

- Give adequate notice concerning the date, time and place of the meeting. Invite only people who need to be there and can contribute to the meeting.

- State the purpose of the meeting clearly. The purpose should be agreed with participants in advance.

- Circulate the agenda in plenty of time before the meeting.

- Book the meeting room and make sure there is adequate seating and tables arranged in the desired fashion. Prepare the paperwork and make sure you have copies available for participants if appropriate.

- Organise a coffee break if the meeting is expected to take a few hours.

- Decide what visuals you will use to help you get your point across. A picture really does speak more than a thousand words! Remember, the characteristics of a good speech can be recalled by the well-known mnemonic FISTIC:

  - Focused
  - Informed
  - Structured
  - Truthful
  - Interesting and
  - Clear.

During

- The function of the chairman is to lead the meeting, control discussion and see that the objectives of the meeting are achieved. The chairman should deal tactfully but firmly with irrelevant contributions. The chairman sticks to the agenda. The meeting should start on time and finish on time. Ideally, an estimated time allocation should be agreed for each item on the agenda. The amount of time given should be in proportion to the priority and importance of each item. These times should be adhered to.

- Encourage open debate. Give everyone an opportunity to express their views. In particular, try and get the shy or quiet participants to contribute their views in order to get a balanced perspective. Control the talkative participants who tend to monopolise a meeting. It is important to summarise frequently.

- Arrive at decisions, ideally by consensus.

- Take the minutes. These are usually taken by the secretary to the meeting. End on a high note.

After

- Finish off writing up the minutes.

- Review how effective the meeting was in terms of achievement of objectives, administration and people attending.

- Circulate action minutes stating what is to be done, who is to do it and by what date. People should be clear on what they have to do.

- Follow up to see that the actions specified have been taken.

The Four P Agenda for Successful Meetings

The Industrial Society's "Four P" agenda for a successful team meeting are:

- **Performance**. Benchmark the team's performance against targets. Compare actual costs against budgets.

- **Policy**. Keep the team informed about company policies that affect them. Relevant new systems, procedures and regulations are always of interest to team members.

- **People**. Appointments, promotions, transfers, and retirements are just some of the "people" issues that are of interest to team members.

- **Points for action**. Review the meeting and assign tasks for action and follow-up. There may be some issues where standards have slipped and corrective action needs to be taken.

Meetings and Group Dynamics

A little understanding of the stages that groups go through when evolving will help you to know what's going on at a meeting.

- **Forming**. This happens at the start of the meeting and is the getting-to-know-you stage. It includes making acquaintances, sharing information, and finding out the relative status of participants at the meeting. Participants discover what kinds of interpersonal behaviours are acceptable and unacceptable at the meeting. People tend to be reserved and suspicious of the intentions of others at this stage.

- **Storming**. This is the confrontational stage. Participants jockey for positions of status within the group. People test out the waters to see how far they will be allowed to go before the chairman intervenes. Discussion may be more open but is often emotionally charged and hostile. Managing conflict takes up a fair bit of time and the meeting may become disorganised and difficult to control. Antagonism may be directed at the chair.

- **Norming**. This is the stage where roles and standards of behaviour have been agreed. Roles such as ideas person, organiser, evaluator, finisher and team worker may become apparent. All these roles are needed for effective meetings. Participants now accept each other and share a common sense of purpose. Compromises are struck, alliances and coalitions formed and the meeting begins to move forward more smoothly.

- **Performing**. This is the stage where the participants get on with the business of the meeting. Disagreements are put aside in the interests of harmony and getting through the business of the meeting expeditiously. Interpersonal relationships between participants are supportive and consensus is facilitated. This helps the meeting to get positive results and achieve its objectives.

If participants at the meeting know each other well, then the stages of forming, storming and norming will not apply. In this instance the meeting will quickly get down to business in an efficient and effective manner. However, if the participants do not know each other then it is very likely that some or all of the four stages will be experienced. The chairman needs to be aware of this and manage the process effectively.

Group Roles

The following group roles are based on the work of Dr Meredith Belbin. These roles determine group effectiveness. In practice, team members can adopt multiple roles. The mnemonic SPECIFIC will help you recall the key roles.

- **Shaper**. The shaper shapes the way the team effort is applied, imposing a pattern on group discussion. The shaper directly influences the decisions and thinking of the team.

- **Plant**. The plant provides the creative ideas for the team. They may be intellectually dominant, solving problems and putting forward new strategies. Their concern for ideas may overshadow their sensitivity to other people's needs.

- **E**valuator. The evaluator is rational and analytical. They stick to the facts. Whereas the plant is good at ideas the evaluator is good at assessing their practicality.

- **C**ompany worker. These are the pragmatists. They get the general ideas and convert them into action plans and programmes.

- **I**nvestigator of resources. This person looks for ideas and resources outside the group to support the team's work. These people are good at networking.

- **F**inisher. They focus the energies of the group to completing the task. They make sure the job is done on time and to a high standard.

- **I**deal team worker. They are very good at maintaining the cohesiveness of the group. They have excellent interpersonal relationship skills, are sensitive to group member's needs and support the group process.

- **C**hairman. The manager of the group. Gets work done through others. Controls and co-ordinates group activities. Has strong leadership skills. Inspires the group with vision and mission statements.

Mentoring

A mentor is usually a senior experienced manager who acts as an advisor, counsellor, encourager, motivator and trusted confidant to an up-and-coming junior manager or young professional. Some companies are using recently retired independent directors to mentor newly appointed directors. Under a government scheme retired senior managers are encouraged to mentor companies in a start-up situation. It is usually a one-to-one relationship.

Ideally, the mentor should be someone other than your line manager. Mentoring is a broader concept than coaching. Coaching tends to be very specific and focused on improving a person's skill in some area such as making presentations to staff or customers. Coaching can be part of mentoring, which has a broader agenda including developing people and identifying suitable staff to fill management succession needs in the future.

In the professions, such as accountancy and engineering, mentoring is often a normal part of the professional training process. The ideal mentor is a person with the interest, experience, time, enthusiasm and will to do the job effectively. The mentor should undertake the job on a voluntary basis. The roles of a mentor can be recalled by the mnemonic CATS:

- **Communicator.** Being a good listener combined with the ability to ask open and closed questions as appropriate is probably the key communication skill that a manager needs to possess to be a good mentor. This includes acting as a sounding board and occasionally as a shoulder to cry on. People know their own problems better than anyone else and half the job of a mentor is to offer a sympathetic ear. Empathy is an essential skill for a mentor who should listen for feelings and emotions in addition to the words. The mentor is there to provide insight, understanding, constructive feedback and put problems in perspective. They are in a position to give independent, non-judgemental and objective viewpoints. The role of a mentor is confidential, like that of a doctor, and should be governed by the equivalent of a Hippocratic Oath. Without this code of practice trust could not be maintained.

- **Advocate** as in Devil's Advocate. In the Devil's Advocate role the mentor will challenge and provoke the staff member to stand back from situations and think about their behaviour and its consequences in a critical and objective way. The mentor may also adopt the role of an Angel's Advocate to encourage creativity and the development of options. They will jointly explore problems and consider possible solutions. However, at the end of the day it is the staff member who is responsible for their own life and decision choices. All the mentor can do is advise and guide in a supportive and non-directive fashion.

- **Trainer.** In this role the mentor will give advice on work issues, job performance, interpersonal relationships, corporate culture, time management, stress management, presentation skills and coping skills. The mentor can help the staff member develop their self-esteem and self-confidence by showing them how to substitute positive thoughts for negative thoughts and feelings. The mentor will have many years' experience of working in the organisation so will be in a good position to offer guidance on how to handle office and organisational politics.

- **Sponsor.** In this role the mentor will advance the interests of the staff member in a fair and equitable way and bring his talents and achievements to the attention of key managers in the organisation. There must be a high degree of trust and mutual regard between the mentor and staff member. The mentor should also be in a position to help them create their own personal vision for professional and career success and guide them towards its achievement. The mentor should put forward the staff member's name for suitable educational, training and development programmes.

Mentoring System

A mentoring system should cover the following:

- *Objectives.* The objective of mentoring is to train and develop people with potential for management positions in the future.

- *Roles.* The role of the mentor is to offer independent and confidential help to young people in the organisation who have potential for development and promotion.

- *Top management support.* The scheme must be supported by the Chief Executive and senior management. Without this support it is likely to die. Mentors should be given proper recognition for the critical role they play in staff development and in identifying talent for management succession. They will need training to carry out their role effectively.

- *Co-ordination.* A responsible senior manager should be appointed to co-ordinate the mentoring scheme and monitor its performance.

- *Performance appraisal.* It should be linked to performance appraisal schemes as a way of identifying people who would benefit from the guidance of a mentor. However, the mentor should not be directly involved in performance appraisal.

- *Selection of mentors.* The success of the scheme depends on the calibre of the mentors selected. It is important that people with time, aptitude, interest and enthusiasm are selected. Choosing managers who have reached their level of incompetence and been pushed sideways will not engender confidence in the mentoring scheme.

- *Implementation of scheme.* Ideally, mentoring agreements should be drawn up to agree expectations and outcomes. If these are known, future misapprehensions and disappointments will be avoided. Both parties should have the option to terminate the agreement at any stage.

- *Monitoring.* The scheme should be reviewed every six months or so, to see how effectively it is operating.

Mentoring Relationships

The possible types of relationships can be recalled by the mnemonic POETIC:

- **P**ublic. The relationship between the mentor and staff member is known widely within the organisation but meetings take place privately and on a confidential basis.

- **O**pen agenda. The style of communication is open and non-judgemental, and any relevant topic can be discussed. Communication is relaxed and the staff member is encouraged to express their views.

- **E**xistence of the mentoring relationship is not widely known within the organisation.

- **T**echnical or formal. The mentoring agreement is in writing to prevent misunderstandings; place and meeting times are scheduled and records are kept of meetings.

- **I**nformal. This is a mutual understanding without any written agreement. Meetings are informal and the staff member is encouraged to approach the mentor casually whenever the need arises.

- **C**losed agenda. The range of topics for discussion are restricted.

The style of relationship chosen should be in line with the needs and culture of the organisation.

Benefits of Mentoring

Benefits of mentoring to the organisation include:

- *Improved training*. Mentoring is a management development tool. It is a method of passing on the experience, wisdom, knowledge, attitudes and skills of senior managers. It is a useful addition to other training approaches and will increase the overall effectiveness and efficiency of training. The mentor becomes the role model for the staff member. Mentoring should be integrated with individual training plans.

- *Reduced staff turnover.* A good mentoring scheme will improve the morale and commitment of staff and reduce staff turnover.

- *Management succession.* Mentoring identifies potential talent for top management positions and trains and develops people to take on these challenging roles in the future.

Benefits of mentoring to the individual:

- *Fast track to skills development.* Mentoring, coaching and on-the-job training are the most effective ways of learning about management. Mentoring should be a part of a formal management development programme. As such it will be part of a systematic approach to skills enhancement of trainees.

- *Self-confidence.* People need other people to help them develop a realistic perspective and find their way in organisations. They often need help to identify and develop their latent abilities. They need advice on how best they might develop their careers, what jobs to consider and what career paths are best suited to their abilities. They need help to resolve personal issues and to cope with the everyday politics and conflicts of organisational life.

- *Company culture acclimatisation.* Culture has been defined as the way a company operates its business and is often expressed in the values, beliefs and attitudes held by the people who work in the company. People need to know what is acceptable behaviour and what is unacceptable in the company. Sometimes this can be quite subtle and needs the guidance and wisdom of an experienced person to pass it on. This is particularly important as part of induction training. Mentoring may play a useful role in acclimatising staff to a new organisation structure as part of a change programme.

Coaching

Coaching is the process where managers systematically give their staff on-the-job training to develop skills, competencies or understanding, through guided practical experiences and regular feedback. Coaching is the way that the knowledge, skills, attitude, experience and wisdom of a manager can be passed on to a staff member. Coaching has more specific and focused goals than mentoring. Coaching is a vibrant part of the learning organisation.

Staff often need coaching in such areas as interpersonal relations, communication skills, problem solving, decision making, creative thinking, teamwork, and delegation. Many of these skills are best learnt on the job on a day-to-day basis as opportunities arise. The process of coaching is informal but planned.

A suggested sequence for coaching could be as follows:

- Identify the present level of knowledge, experience and competence of the person to be coached. A good idea might be to identify the learning style of the learner in addition to your own learning style. For example, if the learner is a reflector and you're an activist you may be at cross-purposes during the coaching session. Obviously, if you can match your learning style with that of the learner the learning process should be helped considerably.

- Agree learning objectives. What desired outcomes will be achieved when the coaching has been completed? The outcomes should be expressed in behavioural terms. What should the person be able to do that they weren't able to do previously? How will you evaluate these outcomes? Draw up a coaching plan. If you are demonstrating a task, sequence the steps in a systematic way. Discuss the background to the task, tell the trainee how to do it, demonstrate the method and then get the trainee to do it. Make sure that you cover no more than eight points during the coaching session, otherwise the learner may suffer from memory overload. Chunking information is based on this principle.

- Set up an appropriate on-the-job situation for coaching. Adopt a non-directive style. The coach should ask questions that help the learner to identify for themselves what the issues are and what the possible solutions might be. Use open questions prefaced by who, what, why, how, when and where to encourage possibility thinking. The manager should also be open to new ideas which the learner might provide. The learning in coaching should be a two-way process.

- Provide non-evaluatory feedback as appropriate. Give the learner space to learn through trial and error while at the same time giving them subtle direction. People learn best by experiencing the repercussions of their own mistakes.

- Summarise the key learning points. Test their understanding by asking questions and by observing actual work practices.

The mnemonic LATE will help you remember the key communications skills that should be used during a coaching session:

- **L**isten. Listening is one of the key skills involved in coaching. Coaching should be a two-way dialogue and not a monologue. Listen carefully to the concerns, feelings, ideas and observations of the learner. Listening of course works both ways and you should check occasionally that the learner has understood what you've said.

- **A**sk questions. Use open questions. These encourage possibility thinking and learning. Avoid closed question which encourage a particular response and rhetorical questions which don't require an answer. These type of questions discourage discussion. Confine yourself to one question at a time. Asking many questions at the same time may lead to confusion. A typical response to multiple questions is that the person answers one question but forgets to respond to the others. Two useful questions are: "What have you learned today?" and "How are you going to use this knowledge in the future?"

- **Test understanding.** You can do this by asking the learner now and again to paraphrase what you've just said. This concentrates the mind of the learner while at the same time checking that questions have been understood and that learning is taking place.

- **Empathise.** Try and visualise what it feels to be the learner. Put yourself in their shoes. A lot of the knowledge and experience you are passing on is at the unconscious competence level as far as you are concerned. However, from the learner's point of view this is all very new to them and it may take some time before they get acclimatised to the new skill. Keep the stages of the learning model in mind: do something, reflect, conclude and do something differently.

The roles adopted by a manager during a typical coaching session can be recalled by the mnemonic SCAM:

- **Supporter.** In this role, the manager facilitates training by providing support in the form of resources such as learning materials and on-the-job and off-the-job learning opportunities.

- **Communicator.** In this role, the manager facilitates discussion, provides training and feedback and offers advice and suggestions for improved performance.

- **Appraiser.** In this role, the manager identifies and agrees the training needed, draws up a coaching plan and monitors and evaluates the outcomes of the coaching process.

- **Motivator.** In this role, the manager motivates the learner to learn by setting challenging goals, praising them for doing things right, encouraging them to take responsibility for their own learning and acting as a role model.

Types of Interviews

There are five interview-type situations in which the manager may be involved. They are selection interviews, counselling interviews, grievance interviews, disciplinary interviews and appraisal interviews. These types of interviews can be recalled by the mnemonic SCALD which stands for:

- **S**election interview

- **C**ounselling interview

- **A**ppraisal interview

- **L**egitimate grievance interview and

- **D**isciplinary interview.

Each of these requires a unique approach but some of the interviewing skills may be common to all.

Selection Interview

This is the assessment and selection of the most suitable person for a particular job vacancy. It may involve interviewing, psychometric testing and the examination of biographical information. The communication style used should be friendly but purposeful.

Conducting the interview:

- The objective is to select the most suitable candidate for the vacant position. It's a question of a correct match between the applicant and the job. You don't want square pegs in round holes and incur the consequent high cost of recruitment and replacement! Plan each stage of the interview. Consider how long it should take. Maintain control over the direction and time taken for the interview. Most interviews take between half an hour and an hour.

- Work from notes — the application form, job description, person profile (see MANIA below) and pre-prepared questions should be close at hand.

- Put the candidate at ease. Use the job description to review the job on offer. Use the application form to help you formulate and structure your questions. Ideally, most of the questions should have been thought out beforehand. Ask open-ended questions prefaced by what, where, why, when and how.

- Avoid closed and leading questions. Do not allow the "halo" or "horn" effect to bias your selection.

Points to watch for can be recalled by the mnemonic MANIA which stands for:

- **M**otivation. Obviously you want to select someone who is a self-starter, can work without direction and will be prepared to pursue further studies if necessary to equip them for promotion in the future.

- **A**cquired qualifications and experience. This will give you a track record by which to gauge whether or not their existing knowledge and experience matches up with the job specification. Qualities such as the ability to work hard, pursue a goal and focus attention on a task can be gauged.

- **N**atural aptitudes. Biographical information such as hobbies may give you a good indication of aptitudes. You may also require candidates to undergo aptitude, IQ, personality and psychometric tests.

- **I**nterpersonal relationship skills. You want to pick someone who will fit in smoothly with the culture, people and work practices of the organisation. Many organisations are now built around teams so an ability to fit in as a member of a team is essential.

- **Ad**justment or maturity. Observing the candidate's appearance, manner and body language and probing for views, values, beliefs and attitudes may give you some help here.

Closing the interview:

- Ask the interviewee if they have any questions.

- Tell the interviewee when they can expect to hear from you.

- Thank the candidate for attending.

After the interview:

- Review your notes and add any further relevant observations.

- Select the candidate that meets the needs of the organisation.

- Check out references, preferably by phone as people are more likely to give information on the phone than by writing.

- Write promptly to all the candidates.

Counselling Interview

Counselling has been defined as the process of helping employees recognise their feelings about issues, define personal problems accurately, find solutions or learn to live with a situation.

Some organisation run formal employee assistance programmes to help staff cope with the anxiety and stress of family, legal and financial problems which may adversely affect on-the-job performance. Others offer an ongoing internal counselling service staffed by welfare officers. Career counselling in the form of life and career planning are run by the more progressive organisations. Outplacement programmes may be run for employees made redundant because of downsizing.

Counselling may also be used to help an employee identify the reasons for some shortfall in job performance. The objective is to change the employee's behaviour so that their job performance will improve. Counselling may come before disciplining. The manager may notice the employee's performance deteriorating in some way and decide to nip the problem in the bud before it develops into a disciplinary matter. The communication style used in counselling should be non-directive and facilitate open discussion. The counselling interview can be considered under three headings:

Before the Counselling Interview

- Keep an open mind on the person and the problem under consideration. Avoid prejudging or stereotyping.

- Prepare to accept that you may be partly at fault. If so, you will need to change your own attitudes and behaviour before you attempt to change the attitudes and behaviour of the employee.

- Write out the purpose of the interview. Your aim is to change the employee's behaviour to improve on-the-job performance.

- Consider an appropriate private venue where you will not be interrupted.

During the Counselling Interview

- Create a friendly and open climate for the interview. Your approach should be that of a facilitator.

- Make sure that your statement about the issue is descriptive and factual rather than judgmental.

- Use reflective listening and appropriate body language to feed back the content and feelings of what is said.

- Get an agreement that the performance is below an acceptable standard and that there is a commitment to improve.

- Establish the cause of the problem by the use of appropriate questions. Open questions are the best to facilitate discussion.

- Agree any changes that should be made and when you expect results. It is best that any changes agreed are at the suggestion of the employee.

- Offer help as appropriate such as training, coaching and further counselling, if necessary. Attendance at a stress management programme may be suggested for someone suffering from job-related stress.

- Set clear interim and final goals and review dates.

After the Counselling Interview

- Follow up on the agreed dates. Compare actual performance against expected standards.

- Praise the improvement, if appropriate, and provide help if targets are not met.

- Reward the achievement of desired standards.

Appraisal Interview

This is an interview to let employees know how they are getting along on the job. The review will investigate the employee's strengths and weaknesses, the reason behind successes and failures and how the employee can improve in the future. Goals for future performance are jointly agreed for review at the next appraisal interview and training and development needs identified. Appraisal interviews are usually held half-yearly or yearly. The following is a brief guide to holding effective appraisal interviews:

Before the Appraisal Interview

- Hold a short preliminary meeting to alert the appraisee of the forthcoming appraisal interview, the proposed content and of the need to prepare for it thoroughly.

- At the preliminary meeting review the agreed goals you set at the last performance appraisal interview. Refer to the previous year's appraisal form. Also refer to any job description if available. Consider targets for the coming year that you would like to have agreed for the appraisal interview. All of this will alert the appraisee of the purpose and scope of the appraisal interview.

- Give plenty notice of place, date and time to the appraisee to attend the interview.

During the Appraisal Interview

- Set the climate for the meeting. The climate, though formal, should be open and non-threatening. Ideally, there should be no surprises at the meeting as the manager will have kept in touch informally with the employee about performance during the year. Appraisal is a continuous process, not a one-off event once or twice a year.

- Invite the appraisee's comments on their performance to get their perspective on issues. The opportunity for self-appraisal should always be given. Give the appraisee plenty of scope to explore and discuss issues.

- Discuss the satisfactory aspects of their performance as well as the unsatisfactory aspects. Use the "hamburger" technique. Start by highlighting achievements, then follow with a discussion of areas requiring improvement and quickly identify another area of job performance that pleases you. Try and emphasise the positive rather than dwell too long on the negative. Criticism, if any, should be constructive rather than destructive.

- Encourage the appraisee to talk and compare actual job performance with the objectives set at the previous year's meeting. Discuss progress towards the achievement of last year's objectives and talk about areas for improvement.

- Jointly set clear goals for the next appraisal interview. Ask the appraisee about concerns, ambitions and career plans for the future.

- Agree training and development needs. Also consider other approaches such as coaching, secondment, project work, job sharing, job rotation and shadowing. Draw up an individual training plan in conjunction with the appraisee. Discuss and agree the appraisal form with the appraisee.

After the Appraisal Interview

- Complete any documentation that needs to be done.

- Implement any training plan. This may be on-the-job or off-the-job or a combination of both.

- Keep copies of appraisal forms and give a copy to the appraisee. These should set out the performance expected of them for the next review period, how it's going to be achieved, how it's going to be measured and the training that will be provided.

- Watch for improved on-the-job performance and praise it if appropriate.

The Performance Potential Model

This model, which is similar to the Growth Share Matrix we saw in the last chapter, will help you to categorise and identify managers with potential or otherwise for promotion. Management succession is a very important aspect of human resource planning. It is an area which is often neglected in practice.

- **Rising stars** are managers with the potential to go further. These managers will benefit from career planning, wider experience and management training. The company may wish to fast track them by rapid promotion, challenging experience and training and development opportunities. However, there should be no such thing as crown princes. It must be stressed to these people that getting into senior management positions takes hard work, loyalty and dedication, competing with others and many years of experience. Only the best will get through to senior management positions.

Performance Potential Model

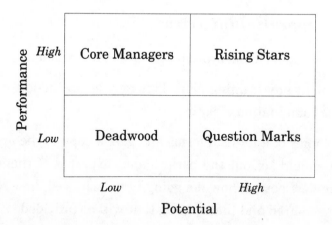

Source: Armstrong (1993).

- **Core managers** are those that the organisation depends on to get things done. They are the backbone of the organisation. They are very good at doing their existing jobs but are considered not to have the potential for further promotion. They will need training to keep their morale high and expertise up to date. It is important to have incentives in place to keep these managers interested and motivated and they should not be taken for granted. The important role they play in the organisation should be acknowledged explicitly.

- **Question marks** are those managers who, for whatever reason, do not seem to be making the grade. They may have the ability but lack the motivation or they may have the motivation but lack the ability. In any event, something should be done about them. Those with the motivation but lacking ability may be brought up to standard by further on-the-job and off-the-job training. Those with the ability but lacking motivation should be encouraged by an appropriate incentive scheme.

- **Deadwood** are managers who have reached the level of their incompetence and are coasting towards retirement. They are the type who have literally retired on the job. They are not good for the company and are blocking rising stars from potential promotional positions. Their negative attitudes may be transmitted to younger managers which is something you don't want to happen. Early retirement might be a solution for those who want to pursue other interests.

Legitimate Grievance Interview

When a member of your staff alleges that the company or you have acted unfairly against them you are dealing with a grievance. Examples might include alleged discrimination, sexual harassment, bullying and breaches of the employment contract. Most companies have a grievance procedure for dealing with staff complaints. Initially, the employee should approach their immediate supervisor or manager. If it remains unresolved, the matter is passed to higher levels of management or to the employee's union. Remember that prevention is better than cure. Most managers do not like handling grievances. However, grievances which are ignored are likely to fes-

ter and explode in your face later on. The grievance process can be
considered in several phases:

Phase one is gathering information:

- If you have an opportunity before the grievance interview, check
  out the facts. Distinguish facts from opinions and assumptions.
  This may give you the chance to nip the problem in the bud
  early on. Grievances can become industrial relations problems if
  left to fester.

- Invite the person to talk. Handle the issue with great diplomacy. Listen with empathy. Attentive silence may be the best
  approach. Your role should be that of a facilitator.

- Actively listen to the grievance by paraphrasing the content and
  feeling of the case. Probe as necessary, but preferably infre-
  quently, to identify the problems and clarify any issues. While
  listening, study body language such as gestures, manner and
  tone of voice. Let the other party let off steam if needed but
  don't let the situation get out of hand.

- Summarising the grievance. This should factually summarise
  the details of the grievance and the person's feelings. Suggest a
  possible solution.

- If an agreed solution cannot be found, adjourn the interview if
  necessary to recheck the facts and reflect on the issues. Agree a
  date and time for a resumed interview.

Phase two is about resolution:

- Give information about your findings. These may be in agreement with the person making the grievance or you may have
  come up with alternative versions of what happened. If the differences are minor it may not prevent resolution of the issue.

- Jointly explore possible solutions. Search for the best solution to
  meet both your needs.

- Agree a resolution of the issue. If it is not possible for a joint resolution, then you may have to impose a solution which you consider the best in the circumstances.

- Follow up to ensure that the action promised has been taken and that the matter has been resolved. Learn from any mistakes made and take steps to make sure that the issue will not arise again in the future.

If there are no grounds for the grievance:

- Discuss with your own manager why the grievance is not valid and get support for your decision. Explain to your manager why the grievance arose in the first place and what steps have been taken to prevent its recurrence.

- Explain to the employee why you are rejecting the claim.

- Listen to reactions but emphasise again why there are no grounds for the grievance. Be firm but fair.

- Explain the appeal process available to the party concerned. This may be to an internal adjudicator or to an external Rights Commissioner.

Disciplinary Interview

If an employee breaches a rule or consistently fails to reach the required level of job performance then a disciplinary situation can arise. Persistent tardiness, unauthorised absences, dishonesty, alcohol or drug abuse, or unacceptable behaviour may give rise to disciplinary action. The employee may be in breach of company rules, the employment contract or the law, such as equality or health and safety legislation. Penalties become increasingly severe as the misconduct is repeated.

The process starts with a verbal warning, followed by a written warning. The written warning should say that if the breach continues then suspension, dismissal or some other penalty may be applied. If the situation persists deductions from pay may arise, bonuses or annual pay increments may be stopped, demotion or indeed suspension from work. If all else fails the ultimate penalty is dismissal from the organisation. The procedure should allow an employee to be accompanied by a work colleague or shop steward if they wish. The disciplinary interview can be considered under the following headings:

Before the Disciplinary Interview

- Consider the purpose of the interview. Decide exactly what you want to achieve. Write down your agenda and objectives for the interview.

- Familiarise yourself with the disciplinary procedure within your organisation. This should be available from your Human Resources Department.

- Be clear about your authority and the support you have. Check this out before the interview.

- Make sure that you check out the facts. Hearsay, assumptions and opinions are insufficient and dangerous to accept at face value. You must be seen to be impartial.

During the Disciplinary Interview

- Get down to business immediately. Avoid "small talk". You need to create a formal climate from the start.

- State the disciplinary offence and listen to the response. Watch for non-verbal language such as manner and tone of voice.

- Summarise and adjourn the interview if necessary to recheck the facts if any doubts arise during the interview.

- Verify the cause of the problem.

- Impose disciplinary measures in line with the company's disciplinary procedure.

- Agree how desired standard of behaviour will be achieved and monitored.

- Offer support and training if appropriate. You must be seen to be firm but fair.

- Agree a review date.

After the Disciplinary Interview

- Record the proceedings of the interview. A written record of all stages is essential.

- Write to the individual setting out the agreed position and the proposed solution.

- Organise agreed help and training.

- Monitor performance at agreed intervals.

- Praise, reward and encourage progress.

Summary

Applying the PICTURE and GRAPEVINE models will help you become a better communicator. PICTURE stands for:

- Pitch

- Inflexion

- Courtesy

- Tone

- Understanding

- Rate

- Enunciation.

The GRAPEVINE mnemonic stands for:

- Gesture

- Recurring pauses

- Appearance

- Posture

- Eye contact

- Voice

- Involve the listener

- Natural self

- Entertaining.

Most of us are not aware just how faulty and limiting our perceptions can be. The ability to ask appropriate questions is a key skill in communications. The FLOOR model is a useful device for helping you recall the right questions. FLOOR stands for:

- Factual questions

- Leading questions

- Open questions

- Overhead questions

- Redirected questions.

The language we use determines how we feel, react to and interpret situations. Being aware of the limitations of the type of language we use should help us become better communicators.

Negotiations, meetings, interviews, mentoring and coaching are common activities in which most managers engage. The POCKET model is a useful device for helping you recall the key steps in any negotiation process. POCKET stands for:

- Planning

- Opening position

- Communicating

- Know your opponent

- Explore options

- Terminate.

Negotiation strategies were considered using the mnemonic SLAP-DASH:

- Salami

- Limited authority

- Apparent withdrawal

- Pretence

- Deadlines

- Acting good guy/bad guy

- Standard practice

- Hand a *fait accompli*.

The various stages that groups go through when at a meeting were discussed such as forming, storming, norming, and performing. Group roles were also explored.

There are many varieties of interviews — selection, counselling, appraisal, grievance and disciplinary — all calling for different approaches and communication skills. The SCALD model will help you recall the various types of interviews:

- Selection

- Counselling

- Appraisal

- Legitimate grievance

- Discipline.

MANIA was discussed as a model for selection criteria. MANIA stands for:

- Motivation
- Acquired qualifications
- Natural aptitudes
- Interpersonal relations
- Adjustment.

Having basic skills in all these areas and the ability to apply them is necessary for success in your career.

Chapter 4 Mind Map

4. COMMUNICATION

Models

PICTURE
- Pitch
- Inflexion
- Courtesy
- Tone
- Understanding
- Rate
- Enunciation

GRAPEVINE
- Gesture
- Recurring Pauses
- Apearance
- Posture
- Eye Contact
- Voice
- Involvement
- Natural
- Entertaining

Perception
- Halo Effect
- Values
- Perceptual
- Stereotyping
- Cognitive Dissonance
- Group Think
- Readiness
- Defense

Conflict
- Grid
- Interpersonal
- Organisational
- Resolving

	Relationships	Task	
Accommodating 1,9	Collaborating 9,9		
	Compromising 5,5		
Avoiding 1,1		Competing 9,1	

Skills
- Negotiation
- Meetings
- Mentoring
- SCALD
- Coaching
- Interviews
  - Selection
  - Counselling
  - Appraisal
  - Legitimate Grievance
  - Disciplinary

Performance Potenial Model

Performance		
Core Managers	Rising Stars	Question Marks
Deadwood		

Potential

Language
- Power
- Questions
- Deletions
- Distortions
- Mind Reading
- Generalisations
- Words
  - Necessity
  - Possibility
- FLOOR
  - Factual
  - Leading
  - Open
  - Overhead
  - Redirected

5. Rapport

"Trust is the lubrication that makes it possible for organizations to work." — Warren Bennis

---

- ◆ *What is rapport?*

- ◆ *How can you practise sensory acuity?*

- ◆ *How can you become a more charismatic person?*

- ◆ *How can you build trust?*

- ◆ *What is the Johari Window?*

- ◆ *What are the different behaviour styles of people?*

Creating Rapport by Remembering Names

The easiest way to create rapport is to use a person's name frequently during a conversation. The sound of a person's name is like music to their ears. Most people find it difficult to remember peoples names. But with a little concentrated effort and practice you can remember the names of those people you want to remember. Just use the well-known MEMORY system as follows:

- • **M**inutes not seconds. When you meet someone for the first time take time to absorb their name. This takes concentrated attention, reflection and practice. Most people are so conscious of themselves, and what they are going to say next, that they fail to hear the other person's name. Ask them to repeat their name, if necessary.

- **E**valuate. Ask questions about the name. Inquire about the name's background. Names usually have a history attached to them. Where did the name originally come from? What does it mean? All these questions will help you to imprint the name on your mind.

- **M**ake an effort. Use the name frequently during the conversation. Make sure you address the person by name when saying your goodbyes. Link the face to the name in a memorable fashion. For example, link the name to a prominent feature of the face. Also, you can link the name to a person you know already with the same name. Imagine in your mind's eye the two people shaking hands with each other.

- **O**rganise by exchanging business cards if these are available. Otherwise write the name into your diary and a few key points about the individual to help you place them in context in the future.

- **R**epeat and review. Occasionally look up your diary and bring the person to mind so that if you meet them again you will remember their name. Use your powers of imagination and visualisation to recall their face and general appearance.

- **Y**our curiosity. Exercise your own curiosity about the person and build up a dossier by inquiring with others who may know something about them. Background family information will help you put the name in context. Look up the telephone number in the directory and see if they are listed. If they are members of a professional body looking up a membership directory will reinforce the name.

Matching Words

Words mean different things to different people. Words are used to describe an experience. However, words are not the experience and our perception of the experience is not reality. Language reflects our thinking. Using the same type of language as the person you are interacting with will build up rapport with that person. Our thoughts are a mixture of mental pictures, sounds and feelings. People have three different states — visual (seeing), auditory (hearing) and kinaesthetic (doing). People tend to have a preference for a particular state. The state a person is in at a particular time can be gauged by the type of words they frequently use.

Visual State

People in a visual state use words and phrases like:

- I see what you mean
- This is something to look forward to
- It colours his view of life
- There is a dark cloud on the horizon
- The future looks bright
- I take a dim view of that
- This looks good to me
- He's a colourful character
- You should put it behind you
- Don't blow it up out of proportion
- The outlook is bleak
- I can see him in my mind's eye
- It was under my nose
- She made a scene

- He's got tunnel vision

- It's clear-cut

- I've got a hazy notion

- I see your point of view

- I'll keep you in the picture.

Auditory State

People in the hearing state use words like:

- He's on the same wavelength

- Turn a deaf ear

- Speak your mind

- He repeated it word for word

- I hear you loud and clear

- What do you say to that?

Kinaesthetic State

People in the doing state use words like:

- I must get to grips with the problem

- Hold on a minute

- He's a cool customer

- You've put your finger on the problem

- They had a heated argument

- He's a smooth operator

- I like to get a feel for the situation

- I'll be in touch.

So the first thing you must do is recognise the state the person is in and match it. Then respond to them using the same type of language whether visual, auditory or kinaesthetic.

You should match in a subtle and sensitive way. Otherwise, instead of building up rapport you could actually cause antagonism. People like people who are like them.

Watching Eye Movements

People tend to look up when they are in a visual state. Looking up to the right means they are creating images while looking up to the left means they are remembering images. People tend to look down when they are in a kinaesthetic state. Looking to the right suggests that they are experiencing feelings and body sensations while looking to the left suggests that they are having an internal conversation. People tend to look sideways when they are in an auditory state. If they are looking to the right it suggests that they are creating words and sounds. Looking to the left suggests that they are remembering words and sounds. So observing a person's eye movements will give you an indication of the type of state they're in. It also improves your powers of observation. You achieve rapport by getting into the same state.

Matching Body Movements

Match the person's body language, posture, gestures and voice tone. Become aware of a person's breathing, skin colour, head angle, facial muscles and even pupil dilation. These are all indicators of a person's present state. Develop your powers of observation. Most of us are so caught up in our own problems that we often fail to notice the external signs that would help us to understand the present state of a person. Generally, a person is either happy, angry or sad. Here again you need to be subtle and sensitive when matching body language. Making it obvious might create discord rather than rapport.

An erect posture might indicate that the person is in a visual state. A swaying posture might indicate that they are in an auditory state while if the person has their head down it might indicate that they are in a kinaesthetic state.

High breathing might indicate that the person is in a visual state. Normal breathing might indicate that they're in an auditory state while shallow breathing might indicate that they are in a kinaesthetic state.

The tone of voice might also indicate the state a person is in. A fast tone of voice might indicate that they're in a visual state. A melodic tone of voice might indicate that they're in a auditory state while a low tone of voice might indicate that they're in a kinaesthetic state.

Becoming aware of all of these in yourself and others will help you to become more observant and understanding. Matching body language will help you to be more in tune with those around you and become better communicators in the process.

Reframing

Empathy is all about visualising what it is like to be in the other person's shoes. You can reframe events by looking at them from a different perspective or seeing them in a different context. There are three points of view:

- Your point of view

- The other person's point of view, and a

- Detached or observer's point of view.

Gandhi, Einstein and Disney were reputed to be very proficient in seeing things from another's point of view. A good marketing professional needs to be able to identify and anticipate customer needs. Generally, successful people tend to have this skill.

Sometimes we are so caught up in a situation that we find it difficult to stand back and look at it objectively and from different viewpoints. You can also reframe the context and content of the situation. You can increase the significance of something by seeing it close up and you can reduce its significance by seeing it small and far away. You can reframe the content by reinterpreting it in a humorous light. The following procedure has proved to be effective with many people:

- Identify the behaviour you want to change.

- Describe it and visualise doing it in your mind's eye.

- Now perfect the behaviour by substituting the new behaviour for the old.

- Anchor it by associating it with an appropriate word or action.

- Run it through like a mental film.

- Rehearse it until it becomes very familiar to you.

Rapport with Yourself

- Develop a sense of inner peace. Your actions should be in harmony with your values and beliefs, otherwise internal conflict arises. Walk your talk. Acknowledge your emotions. People become unhappy when their minds are out of tune with the actions of their body. Doing things at odds with your conscience causes stress. The greater the degree of physical and mental rapport the greater your well-being and the healthier you are likely to feel. Doing a job which no longer interests you is a common example of being out of rapport with yourself.

- Live in the present moment. That's all you have. The past is gone. The future is not yet here. You are only guaranteed the present. So enjoy the moment! Life is not a dress rehearsal. The past is history. The present is reality. The future is a mystery.

- Reserve some time each day to be on your own. You might use this time for some meditation or indeed just to relax and listen to your favourite music.

- Recognise your intuition. Get in touch and listen to your feelings. This will give you excitement, enthusiasm, concentration, charisma and personal power. In the western world we are too heavily into logic and analysis. After all, when Henry Ford pursued his dream to make transport available to the masses he wasn't operating on the basis of logic but solely on the bases of feelings and intuition. In fact, most of the breakthrough discoveries in the world were as a result of feelings, intuitions and dreams rather than logic and analysis. Many of the ideas were pursued even when held up to fierce criticism and ridicule. Market researchers concluded that there would be no demand for the Sony "Walkman", yet it has proved to be one of the most successful products of all time.

- Change your inner dialogue. Feel good about yourself by using positive inner dialogue. Changing your inner thoughts will change your outward actions and behaviour. Decide to run your own mind. Do not let other people run it for you. Other people should not influence or be the cause of your moods. Your imagination is your greatest resource. You can decide whether to be happy, angry or sad. You can anchor a particular positive state by associating it with a particular word or action. By recalling the particular word or action you can associate it with the desired state at will. States are contagious. People like to be around people who make them feel good about themselves. Use your body language and words to build rapport with others.

Remember that you can change your state at will. You are responsible for your own thoughts and feelings and you can control them.

- Know your sense of place in creation. Realise you belong to a larger whole. You are a spiritual being in a human body; when your body dies your spirit lives on. We are all part of the earth's ecological system, all interconnected to each other and to the earth. Relax. Peace and quietness allows access to inner wisdom.

- You must be capable of loving yourself before you can love others. A basic tenet of Christianity is: "love thy neighbour as thy self." Aristotle tells us that if all people were friends, justice would not be necessary, for if they loved those whom they thought admirable, they would be benevolently disposed toward them.

Building Trust

Trust is the faith and confidence that people place in each other. Without trust there can be no rapport. As a manager you will not achieve trust automatically; you must earn it by walking your talk. Managers who on the one hand tell the workforce that they are essential to the success of the company, and on the other hand implement business process reengineering with its emphasis on downsizing and cost reduction, are unlikely to be trusted.

Trust is a two-way process. If managers do not trust employees then employees will not trust managers. Managers can demonstrate trust by investing in the development of their people and delegating challenging tasks to staff and keeping them informed of what is going on in the company.

Unfortunately, many managers operate to the "mushroom" theory of management: they keep staff in the dark and feed them plenty of manure. Other managers have often been accused of being deceitful and dishonest — the "kipper" theory of management: two-faced and no guts!

Many an industrial relations dispute is caused by mistrust on both sides. It emanates from a "them-and-us attitude". Many managers see workers as lazy, irresponsible and untrustworthy. On the other hand, many workers see managers as more interested in playing politics, deceitful and out to feather their own nests.

Trust may take years to build up and one betrayal can cause staff to lose trust in their manager. Trust is considered by many to be one of the most important ingredients in successful leadership, and also the most vulnerable. Staff may not always agree with the decisions of managers but they will trust those who tell the truth, keep their promises, uphold their interests and support them in their hour of need.

Staff will not give their best efforts for a manager who they do not trust. The work climate may deteriorate. People become suspicious of one another, information is withheld, facts are often distorted, deception is the norm and interpersonal relationships are poor. The standing and credibility of a manager is partly determined by how trustworthy they are perceived to be by staff and indeed other stakeholders such as customers, suppliers and shareholders.

After the Watergate scandal Richard Nixon was no longer seen to be trustworthy by the American public, one of the stakeholders, and was forced to resign. In the church some clergy have been found guilty of molesting children which is a serious breach of trust and contrary to their vows of chastity. These revelations have encouraged many to turn their backs on organised religion. In marriage, trust is possibly the most important ingredient of a successful marriage. When trust is gone, the marriage deteriorates and eventually breaks down. Similarly in business when companies lose the trust of their customers they will vote with their feet and take their business elsewhere. Ultimately, without the trust of customers, companies will fail to survive in the marketplace.

The Trust–Control Dilemma

How much of the work that a manager is responsible for should be done personally and how much should be delegated to other staff? That is the basic question of the trust-control dilemma. The more trust a manager has in an employee the more that will be delegated. Charles Handy expressed the problem in an equation: $T + C = Y$ where T is trust, C is control and Y is a constant. An increase in T means more trust and less control and more delegation. An increase in C means more control, less trust and less delegation. The dilemma is to get the right balance between trust and control. Managers are often reluctant to delegate because they retain responsibility for the work of their area. Delegation presupposes that the people to whom you delegate are willing, able and experienced to do the work passed on. If these conditions are not present delegation will fail.

The Johari Window

The Johari Window was designed to help people understand how they interact with others and how disclosing personal information can improve rapport. Johari is named after the creators of the model, Joe Luft and Harry Ingram. The Johari window is a two-by-two table that contrasts areas of public and private information about an individual.

The first box of the window is known as the public area. This represents information known to both self and others. This information includes a person's manner of speech, marital status, and favourite pastimes. This is the type of information that facilitates communication and rapport. According to the model, the more information that is in the public area the greater the degree of rapport. This requires a great deal of trust.

The second box of the window is the blind area. Information in this box is known to others but not to yourself. For example, it might be known to staff that their manager is usually in a bad mood early in the morning but by the afternoon his mood has improved for the better. So if they want to get approval for something the best time to look for it is in the afternoon. People with large blind areas can be difficult to deal with. They are often grumpy and insensitive to others. They often lack rapport and can be manipulated by others.

The Johari Window

Your View on Yourself

	Known	Unknown
Known	Public Area	Blind Area
Unknown	Closed Area	Unknown Area

Other's View of You

The third box of the window is the closed area. It represents information known to yourself but not shared with others. This area may include personal feelings about others, your opinion about the boss and information about one's personal life. People keep information in the closed area because they feel that disclosure would damage their reputation and undermine their position. Where trust in an organisation is low, then the closed area will be large, and the public area will be small. On the other hand, where trust is high in the organisation, the closed area will be small and the public area will be large.

The fourth box of the window is called the unknown area. Information in this box is unknown to oneself and others. It includes unconscious motivations, repressed feelings, and past memories. Some psychologists believe that information from the unknown area has an important impact on the ways people behave in all areas. In the US the A.K. Rice Institute offers group relations workshops designed to help people understand the unconscious ways in which they respond to issues of power, authority and gender within organisations.

The Johari Window and Personal Development

Obviously the Johari Window can be very useful as a personal development tool. When we meet people for the first time we are reluctant to disclose much about ourselves and the open window is very small. As trust develops we disclose more and more about ourselves. Our background, history, beliefs and attitudes become known. Thus the open window becomes larger and the closed window becomes smaller.

To increase the open window further it is necessary to reduce the blind area. This can be achieved by being more open and honest and by seeking and accepting feedback from other people. As the open area grows and the hidden and blind areas diminish, it is likely that the unknown area will reduce as well. This will lead to greater self-awareness and rapport with others.

Most organisations encourage the expansion rather than the contraction of the closed area. Companies tend to hire hands rather than hearts and show only superficial concern for people's personal and domestic lives. They expect you to do your job, collect your pay, keep your mouth shut and keep your troubles to yourself. Dealing with personal issues is viewed as a minefield.

The Johari Window and Group Development

Another use of the Johari Window is to describe how work groups evolve. When people first meet their public areas are likely to be small and their closed areas large. Their blind areas may also be large. However, as the group develops and trust increases the public area will increase. Others, too, will be more willing to provide information so that individual's blind areas become smaller. The greater the public area, the greater the degree of harmony and cohesiveness in the group. The Johari Window can be correlated with the stages of group evolution — forming, storming, norming and performing.

Different Strokes for Different Folks

People are different. They bring different experiences and backgrounds to a problem and thus develop different perspectives. To be a successful manager you must be sensitive to these differences and adapt your managerial style to cater for them. If you do so you will develop greater understanding and rapport with your staff. The mnemonic TOPMOST will help you recall the different behaviour styles of people:

- **Towards–away.** People are motivated in different ways. *Towards* people know what they want and are motivated towards goals and objectives. *Away* people are motivated away from things they want to avoid such as pain and discomfort. A towards person will talk about what they want. An away person will talk about what they don't want. Away people are good at finding problems but not very good at coming up with solutions. They make good controllers. Towards people are problem solvers with plenty of initiative. They are the type of people in high demand in modern business.

- **Options–procedures.** *Options* people are creative. They think laterally and easily generate alternatives. They like coming up with new ways of doing things. They will take an existing procedure and suggest ways of making it more efficient. Options people need plenty of variety. On the other hand, *procedures* people like operating to rules and regulations. They are distressed by change. They make good bureaucrats so don't expect them to come up with novel solutions! They make excellent administrators where the work is predictable and routine. They tend to seek out predictable careers such as the Civil Service.

- **Proactive–reactive.** *Proactive* people plan ahead and think about the future. *Reactive* people react to problems as they arise and think about the past. Proactive people are always thinking about efficiencies and how quality can be improved. They identify their own training needs and draw up their own training and development plans. They make good strategic thinkers. Reactive people love to be immersed in problems and make good operational staff.

- **Maintenance–task.** Some people are focused on the task and forget about human relations. Others focus more on people issues and are very good at relating to others in the team. There should be a role for each type of person in any team. The *task* person will make sure that the job gets done on time, while the *maintenance* person will make sure that the needs and sensitivities of people are catered for.

- **Outside–inside reference.** People with an internal reference know instinctively when they have done a good job. They don't have to be told by their boss how they're performing on the job. They do not rely on others for emotional support or approval. They are entirely independent, self-sufficient and self-reliant. They are internally motivated. People with an external reference need the boss to tell when they've done a good job. They need mental strokes from other people such as praise and appreciation. Many people working in organisations are externally referenced. They need a structure such as management by objectives or similar appraisal system to let them know how they are getting along in their jobs.

- **Self–others.** *Self* people are introverted and are more concerned with their own feelings rather than the feelings of others. As a result they may come across as insensitive to the needs of others. They make good researchers. *Others* people are extroverted and are constantly switched into the needs of others. They make good trainers, human resource people, salespeople, health care professionals and public relations people.

- **Things–people.** Some people are good at *things* — they prefer to be dealing with machines and systems rather than people. They make good engineers and programmers. But keep them away from people! There are others who are naturally good at dealing with people. They like to talk and are good when interacting socially with others. These *people* people will be sensitive to customers' needs and would also be good in a human relations role.

Summary

Rapport is feeling in harmony with yourself and with others. Remembering people's names is a great way to achieve rapport with others. The mnemonic MEMORY was suggested as a useful tool to help you to recall names. This stands for:

- Minutes not seconds

- Evaluate

- Make an effort

- Organise

- Repeat

- Your curiosity.

Rapport can be achieved by matching your words and body language to that of others. Internal rapport is necessary for harmony and peace of mind. Reframing is a technique for evaluating past experiences and reinterpreting them in a more favourable light. Your imagination is the greatest resource that you have.

The Johari Window was discussed as a technique to become more open with others. It can be used to improve personal and group effectiveness.

The different behaviour styles of people can be recalled by the mnemonic TOPMOST:

- Towards–away

- Options–procedures

- Proactive–reactive

- Maintenance–task

- Outside–inside reference

- Self–others

- Things–people.

Knowing the natural preferences of people will help you to build up rapport with them more easily.

Chapter 5 Mind Map

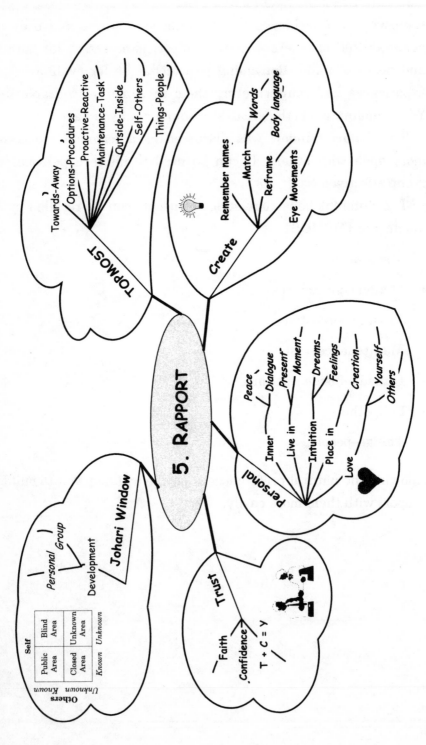

6. Ideals

"The character ethic, which I believe to be the foundation
of success, teaches that there are basic principles of
effective living, and that people can only experience
true success and enduring happiness as they learn and
integrate these principles into their basic character."
— Stephen R. Covey

♦ *What is ethics?*

♦ *Why is ethics important?*

♦ *Who monitors ethical standards?*

♦ *Why is ethics training necessary?*

♦ *What standards should you follow?*

♦ *Where is ethics relevant?*

Honesty is the Best Policy

Honesty is the best policy and the truth shall prevail. This principle is just as relevant to organisations as it is to individuals. Principles are deep, fundamental truths that have universal application. People who do not live by guiding principles are likely to reap the consequences. Yet all we have to do is look at the daily newspapers to see that this maxim is not universally adopted and that cheating and lying is prevalent in politics and business. Lying is euphemistically referred to as being economical with the truth as if this justifies the practice.

Presidents have fallen because of poor moral and ethical standards. Chief executives have been forced to resign from their exalted positions and some even have been jailed. Employees at all levels have been unethical and many have paid the consequences of major setbacks in their careers, prosecution, incarceration and total disgrace. Some clergy have abused their positions of trust with cases of child abuse, paedophilia and the misappropriation of church funds. Banks have been found to be less than honest with their customers. Some politicians have been found to have taken bribes, euphemistically referred to as cash gifts, and even the police have not escaped scandal in this regard.

The practice of good ethics makes an important contribution to an organisation's success. Ethics and people go together. Organisations have no conscience. It is the people who work for an organisation who determine its ethical standards. So people can destroy themselves and their organisations by adopting poor ethical standards.

Ethics are moral principles or rules of conduct that guide people in their dealings with others. Business ethics is about honesty, trust, respect and fairness. There are five basic sources of values influencing people in business: religious, philosophical, cultural, legal and professional. We will particularly deal with the philosophical, legal and professional sources in this chapter. The five basic sources of ethics are shown on the following page.

When managers make decisions affecting stakeholders they must obey the law and be guided by basic humane ethical principles such as honesty, truthfulness, integrity, fairness and justice. The internal stakeholders include managers and employees. The external stakeholders include unions, customers, competitors, suppliers, lenders, shareholders, government, local authorities, local communities and the general public.

All of these groups are affected by management decisions and expect ethical treatment. It is from this broad stakeholder perspective of internal and external stakeholders that we will consider ethics in an organisation.

Five Basic Sources of Ethics

The Importance of Character

Many people are guided by their instincts rather than principle. If you don't know what you stand for you will fall for anything. A person's character is the sum and substance of all their thoughts. People of character are kind, honest, trustworthy, faithful, self-controlled and responsible. They have personal integrity and keep their promises. Living a principled life must be practised with discipline. Habits are a disposition to do acts of a certain kind. Aristotle said we are what we repeatedly do. You can control your thoughts, actions and therefore your habits. Choose to be of noble character and you will be a success in life. Heraclitus, a sixth century Greek philosopher, wrote, "a man's character is his fate".

The incidence of dishonesty, theft, bribery, cheating, lying, self-interest, abuse of power, corruption, price fixing, conflicts of interest, insider dealing and so on is very prevalent in modern society. For example, in the public sector employees are allowed seven days casual sick leave with pay without a doctor's certificate. These days can be availed of up to two at a time. It is common practice with some people, who are perfectly healthy, to call in sick, treating the days as an extension of annual leave and an entitlement. This is deceit and stealing an employer's time and money.

Other people think nothing of stealing small items of stationery such as pens and pencils from their employer or making personal telephone calls and not paying for them. Staff see their managers take unnecessary business trips overseas as a free holiday or driving when they could use the train in order to get the mileage allowance. People must know that these things are wrong but yet have no qualms of conscience about it. These are the symptoms of a general decline in moral standards and character in business and throughout society.

Religious, politicians, civil servants, businessmen and the general public have all been tainted. Even trainers of sporting and athletic associations and social workers have been tainted by reports of sexual abuse. Furthermore, sports competitors have been found to have taken drugs to enhance performance.

Poor ethical standards do not pay. The Law of Cause and Effect states that for every action there is a compensatory reaction. In other words, you sow what you reap. Even though you may feel that trickery and dishonesty pay, this is not so and unprincipled characters usually come to a bad end. In the EU the unethical past of a former prime minister of one of the member states has now come to haunt him in his days of retirement, which should be a time of tranquillity and public adulation rather than a time of hassle and shame. He has been hounded by the media and the taxation authorities, and has had to endure the shame of appearing before a judicial enquiry. An otherwise illustrious career is now in shambles because of media revelations of alleged corruption, abuse of power and bribery while in office. To quote Thomas Babington Macaulay, "the measure of a man's real character is what he would do if he knew he never would be found out".

What is Ethics?

Ethics has been studied and written about since the time of the Greek philosophers. Later, the religious teachings of Judaeo-Christianity, Buddhism, and Islam all concur on not hurting people, not stealing and not lying. These precepts form the basis for most legal systems.

One of the basic tenets underlying ethical conduct is to "do unto others as you would have them do unto you". This golden rule is found among many religions and, if practised, would solve a lot of ethical problems in personal and business life. You can hurt people as much by word as by deed. Consider the prevalent practice of character assassination. Better to follow the precept that if you have nothing nice to say about someone then say nothing. Better still, if you feel you have to say something about someone then make it your practice to substitute complimentary remarks for derogatory remarks.

Ethics is an attempt to determine moral standards or rules that ought to govern human conduct, the values worth adopting, and the character traits worth developing in personal living. Therefore, ethics attempts to see what rules, codes, values, and standards ought to be adopted for morally right behaviour, integrity and truthfulness in human situations. Ethical systems, even in different cultures, virtually all accept that any action injurious to another is wrong.

Ethical behaviour in business can be encouraged by a code of business ethics — a guide to human behaviour. However, a code in itself does not guarantee ethics. You can follow a company code of ethics and still be unethical. It is impossible to cover every possible situation in a code of ethics or for that matter in legislation. At the end of the day, people must be guided by their conscience as to what is right and wrong. Some of the major companies in which scandals happened had a formal code.

Ethics is an evolving process. Through the exercise of conscience human beings naturally adopt ethical principles. These have been refined through generations of experience, and put into context by philosophy and religion. We regard them as fundamental and essential. But human experience changes and develops. Thus the question of how to apply external principles to new developments in society needs working on. Applied philosophy, like creation, is evolving.

Consider that in the comparatively recent past, few people worried about equality or economic rights for women, segregation was accepted in the US and, more recently, apartheid in South Africa. Sectarianism and discrimination were rife in Northern Ireland in housing, employment and job selection. In many countries people without property could not vote, and there was wholesale corruption in business and government.

Stakeholder Issues

Today, some of the major ethical issues facing business include equality, sexism, ageism, the disabled and the environment. Because of unawareness and lack of training in ethics, pure greed and abuse of power, managers sometimes make unethical decisions in relation to their stakeholders.

Issues in relation to internal stakeholders include health and safety, right to privacy, equality, sexual harassment, selection, redundancy, pay, working conditions, insider dealing and conflict of interest. Issues for external constituents include environmental protection, unfair competition, safe consumer products, price-fixing, bribery, corruption and advertising. It is generally accepted that relations with external stakeholders cause more ethical conflict than relations with internal stakeholders.

Some of the issues relating to external stakeholders are quite complex such as environmental issues. Examples of these include the various issues and ethics involved in such areas as chlorofuoro-carbons (CFCs), asbestos, the ozone layer, toxic waste, lead in petrol, plastic bags, fish kills, acid rain, electro-magnetic fields, genetically-modified foods and so on. Waste disposal management is now an important area for most organisations.

Common Topics for Codes of Ethics

While the areas covered in codes vary from one industry and company to another some common topics include:

- Honesty and legal compliance

- Product safety and quality

- Health and safety at work

- Conflicts of interest

- Employment practices

- Marketing and advertising

- Financial reporting

- Supplier relationships

- Pricing, invoicing and contracting

- Insider dealing

- Bribery and gifts

- Use of privileged information

- Environmental protection

- Political contributions

- The award of contracts

- Equality issues.

The BIM Code of Ethics

The British Institute of Management code of ethics recommends that managers should:

- Take account of the interest of others

- Never maliciously injure the professional reputation or career prospects of others

- Declare personal interests which may conflict with company interests

- Be concerned with the health, welfare and safety of all

- Respect confidentiality

- Not accept gifts

- Public communications made should be true and not misleading.

Ethics and Power

It seems that fame and fortune often breed arrogance and a sense of invulnerability that one is above the law. The higher a person rises in an organisation, the more self-confident they become. Along with self-confidence and seniority comes less and less control. Together these can lead to overconfidence and a contempt for others, which is a deadly cocktail for the company. Robert Maxwell raided the pension fund to keep his corporate empire afloat. This unethical practice and abuse of power caused financial distress and ruin to pensioners.

As people become more powerful they sometimes lose touch with those beneath them and their sense of reality becomes distorted. As power becomes absolute, there is less respect for others and less need for their friendship and support. Also, there is less need for influencing others. Reliance is solely on the exercise of position power. Such people don't suffer fools gladly and become arrogant, domineering and conceited. Since people with a lot of power don't need others they take control of all decision making, undermining even further the power of people below them.

The abuse of power is not inevitable in the case of executives who exercise their power in an ethical fashion. When power tactics and political behaviour influence behaviour for the good of the organisation as a whole, then such behaviour is ethical. However, unethical political activity benefits the individual and is detrimental to the organisation. The exercise of power should be respectful of individual rights such as the right to privacy, courtesy, respect and fairness.

Why Ethics?

Ethics has always been an issue in business. These days because of modern business sophistication and, in particular, the complex and changing environment, ethics is more important, topical and relevant. Recent ethical scandals in the church, government and business, at home and abroad, have also highlighted the need for vigilance and control mechanisms.

Good ethics is good business. It leads to repeat sales, lower employee turnover, good reputation and consistent behaviour. On the other hand, unethical practices have ruined individuals and whole businesses. Spooner (1992) mentions a study involving some 1,400 senior executives in 14 countries who were asked to rank the personal qualities of the ideal CEO in the year 2000. The highest ranking went to ethics. The figure below shows how good ethics pays:

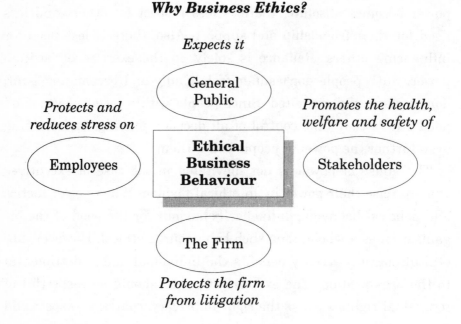

Why Business Ethics?

Expects it

General Public

Protects and
reduces stress on

Promotes the health,
welfare and safety of

Employees

Ethical Business Behaviour

Stakeholders

The Firm

Protects the firm
from litigation

Survey of Ethics

Poor ethics is prevalent in business. Hoffman and Moore (1990) refer to a 1984 Survey of Fortune 500 largest industrial corporations by the Centre for Policy Research. Roughly two-thirds had been involved in illegal behaviour over the previous ten years. The survey did not include unethical acts as judged by prevailing moral standards. It focused exclusively on illegal acts. These included price-fixing, overcharging, violation of environmental laws, bribes, fraud, patent infringement and antitrust laws. It would have shown an even worse outcome if unethical acts were included. The figure below shows how unethical behaviour is counterproductive.

Unethical Behaviour Becomes Counterproductive

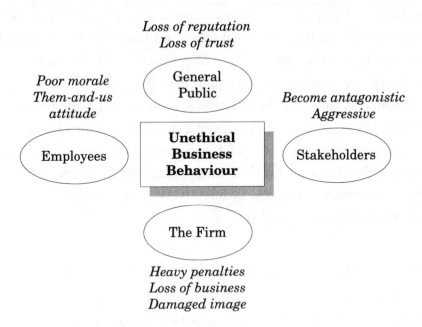

A survey conducted for the Market Research Society in England in January 1988 asked the following question: "How do you rate the standards of honesty among each of the following"? The results were:

	High (%)	**Low (%)**	**No View (%)**
Doctors	83	2	15
Police	62	7	31
Television and radio	47	10	43
The City	22	24	54
MPs	18	23	59
Top businessmen	17	29	54
National newspapers	12	41	47

This shows that business has a very poor ethical image in relation to other professions.

In politics, scandals such as Watergate in the US and bribery/ corruption in Japan have brought down presidents, governments and financial institutions. Good ethics, on the other hand, contributes to a business's success. On a cost–benefit analysis basis, it can be shown that good ethics more than pays its way.

Nothing is worse to the image of a company than poor ethics in relation to customers, suppliers and the public. Nothing damages a company more in the eyes of their customers than poor ethical practice. On the other hand, nothing enhances the image of a company more than to be seen to have good ethics in all its dealings with all its stakeholders.

Monitoring Standards — The Media

Watchdog bodies, such as consumer and environmental groups that monitor the activities of companies in their dealings with customers and the environment, expect companies to be ethical in their business operations. Cover-ups are no longer acceptable. The public is demanding accountability and transparency in political and business dealings. Good ethics is good public relations. Furthermore, the media such as the press, television and radio are only too ready to expose unethical practice in business, politics and the church.

The financial services area has received a lot of media attention with respect to ethical issues. The issues which have attracted most attention include:

- Insider dealing

- Fraud and embezzlement

- False accounting

- Improper use of company funds

- Forgery

- Inadequate controls

- Bribery

- Concealing relevant facts

- Breach of covenants

- Tax evasion and avoidance.

Some of the leading companies world-wide have been involved in financial scandals. In Ireland, some of the banks are currently (1999) under investigation by the Government for loading interest charges onto customers' accounts without first seeking their permission and tax evasion on offshore customer deposit accounts. This practice was defrauding customers and the exchequer.

There are allegations of mis-selling in the life assurance industry. Mis-selling is the practice of "churning". This involves persuading customers to cash in existing policies and opening new ones. This means that virtually another whole year's premium payments went to sales staff and not to the enhancement of the value of a customer's policy. Customers lose out because 90 per cent of first-year premiums go in commissions and costs. Opening a new policy incurs a second round of commission charges reducing the capital saved.

Lord Acton felt that power corrupts and that absolute power corrupts absolutely. Is it therefore a question of abuse of power, poor moral standards or a lack of adequate checks and balances?

Outside the finance area, some internationally famous cases include Union Carbide's Bhopal disaster, Chernobyl, the Dalkon Shield, Nestlé's Infant Formula, the Alaskan Oil Spill and BCCI. In recent times the cigarette industry has come in for major criticism because of attempts in the past to hide research findings which showed just how carcinogenic and detrimental to health smoking was. Many consumers have taken legal action for compensation for injury to health against tobacco companies. Some of these have been successful and others are in progress.

Double Standards

In the Bhopal tragedy in 1984 poor safety, maintenance, inadequate training standards and cost-cutting measures were at the core of the problem. More than 3,000 people died and more than 200,000 were injured when toxic gas seeped from Union Carbide's insecticide plant. The Bhopal episode cost Union Carbide at least $470 million, the amount that was paid to the Indian Government as compensation. The lax standards in Bhopal would not have been tolerated in the parent company in the US.

Different standards were acceptable and tolerated outside the US. The location of a potentially dangerous chemical plant in a densely populated area also could not be justified. The Indian Government was also remiss in allowing large populations to continue to settle in close proximity to the plant. The regulatory framework such as health and safety legislation in third world countries is often inadequate or non-existent. Tobacco companies have no qualms about pushing cigarettes in these countries.

The Velsicol Chemical Company of Chicago, manufacturers of a pesticide called Phosvel, is another example of the practice of double standards. The World Health Organisation classified this product as extremely dangerous due to its delayed neurotoxic effects — it could cause paralysis for some time after exposure. Phosvel was not approved for sale in the US by the Environmental Protection Agency. However, Velsicol sold it to developing countries where there were no import restrictions.

Consider the Alaskan Oil Spill, which was caused by the grounding of the Exxon oil tanker *Valdez* in Alaska. The accident was caused by an inadequately trained crewman steering the tanker. In the meantime, the captain, who had been drinking, was below deck. Some time previous to the incident the captain had been disqualified for drunken driving, nevertheless he was deemed okay to skipper a ship!

A ferry called *The Herald of Free Enterprise* sunk off Zeebrugge with a loss of 193 lives when it sailed with its bow door open. Bad employment practices, undermanning, alcoholism and poor communications between management and staff were some of the findings of the Sheen Enquiry. There was an outcry from the public and a demand that the directors be charged with corporate manslaughter.

Irrespective of the law, the basic universal ethical principle of "do unto others as you would have them do unto you" should apply. In the case of Bhopal and Velsicol this principle was ignored. Different standards for different cultures is unsatisfactory. In the case of Exxon, low personal and corporate ethical standards prevailed.

Companies with overseas branches are often faced with ethical issues when local practices differ from home. What should they do when officials expect bribes to secure contracts, or when confronted with exploitation of child and female labour in the third world? The traditional response — when in Rome, do as the Romans do — is no longer acceptable.

Positive Ethics

On a more positive note some companies now take safety and ecological issues very seriously. For example, Honda and others now have many advanced car features. These include airbag and anti-lock braking systems, exhaust emission systems for air pollution control, safety features, and various fuel economy improvement technologies. In addition, they use other environmental and health protection technologies such as recycling and non-CFC refrigerant or non-asbestos materials.

Many companies are responding to environmentalism, consumerism and media attention by adopting green issues in marketing. Some even make it an unique selling proposition. For example, in response to the "lead in petrol issue" car manufacturers now offer catalytic converters as standard car features. Also, in response to consumerism and the safety lobby all cars have seat belts fitted, most have ABS brake systems, many have side impact bars, air bags for the driver's and front passenger's protection, and other safety features.

Volvo emphasises the safety feature of its cars as their unique selling proposition. McDonalds has discontinued the use of CFCs in fast food cartons. Furthermore, all the aerosol manufacturers have phased out the use of CFCs. In the UK, the Body Shop is committed to ecological issues and animal rights. Some supermarkets offer alternatives to the use of plastic bags which are non-biodegradable and a major source of pollution. In the area of food they offer free range chickens and eggs and vegetables grown organically. In response to customer demand, genetically modified foods are now being clearly labelled.

The increasing need for ethical awareness and sensitivity in making decisions, combined with the greater employee numbers who make them, is motivating companies to take an interest in developing codes of business ethics and training programmes.

Monitoring Standards — Environmental Groups

The Green Movement is a powerful political lobby whose remit is to protect the environment. Most EU member states now have a Green Party and have some parliamentary representation. Movements such as Greenpeace, Earthwatch and Friends of the Earth actively monitor the potential damage done by businesses and government to ecological systems and the environment.

The destruction of the ozone layer, the accelerating loss of tropical forests, the growing amount of waste from excessive packaging and consumption and intensive farming are just some of the problems demanding urgent attention. Polluted seas, radiation leaks, nuclear waste, oil spillages from tankers at sea, acid rain, electromagnetic fields, fish kills and the greenhouse effect are popular "green" issues receiving media coverage.

Monitoring Standards — Animal Welfare

The Animal Liberation Movement (ALM) promotes the rights of animals. It seeks to end all unnecessary cruelty and suffering inflicted by humans on animals, especially in scientific experimentation, product testing, cosmetics and in food production. It advocates vegetarianism and alternative methods of research and experimentation.

Although normally peaceful, using such methods as boycotting and lobbying, some elements of the ALM have resorted to violence from time to time. Department stores in the centre of London have been firebombed. In Ireland, they are trying to stop hare coursing. A few years ago one of the major department stores in Dublin discontinued stocking fur coats because of threats. These examples show how important it is for managers to have a wide perspective on ethical issues when making business decisions. It also highlights the need for ethics training, which is not currently a priority in most organisations.

The meat and animal products industries rely on intensive factory farming methods, which many consider cruel. For example, the intensive rearing of hens raises many ethical issues. They are usually packed into crowded cages, unable to move and as a result suffer foot damage and other injuries. Birds are "debeaked" to prevent pecking injuries and cannibalism. Veal calves fare worst. To produce gourmet "milk-fed" veal, new-born calves are taken from their mothers. They are then chained in small crates. Here they spend their entire lives in total darkness. To increase weight and prevent muscle development, they are not allowed to exercise. Growth stimulators and antibiotics cause chronic diarrhoea.

Managers of these factory animal farms are not naturally cruel but are driven by business considerations, such as the need to make profits, rather than ethical considerations. In addition, the danger to humans from the ingestion of growth hormones and antibiotic residue should be a concern. What effects have these on our health? Obviously, there are many other factors besides profits that should be taken into account by managers. In the last few years the incidence of BSE or Mad Cow disease and the embargo on cattle exports from Britain has highlighted the need for vigilance.

How is Ethics Implemented?

Ethics should be linked to the values and ethos of the company, its HRM policy, vision statement, corporate philosophy, strategic objectives and, ultimately, its mission. Basically, it should be compatible with generally acceptable standards of honesty, integrity, fairness and decency.

Therefore, the motivation for companies to implement an ethics policy, apart from compliance with the law, protection against employee misconduct and maintaining a reputation for integrity, is pursuance of a well thought-out, ethical corporate philosophy.

Any ethical programme must have the support of top management who should lead by example. Awarding huge salary increases to themselves while at the same time expecting employees to take pay cuts or forego increases is not exactly leading by example. The ethical message must be communicated to all staff by word and by deed. It is insufficient for managers just to be going through the motions. Values are caught more often than taught. We are all role models because we are continually setting an example, whether good or bad. Managers must be seen to "walk the talk" as well.

A company code should be drawn up with specific codes for functional departments. It is only in the latter that the particular issues relevant to, say, the needs of the finance, marketing and purchasing departments can be addressed.

Ethics Training

Training would be a vital ingredient of any ethics programme. Studies carried out in the US show that 80 per cent of the largest corporations there have taken some initiative to instil ethics in their employees. In addition, 44 per cent of those corporations provide employees with some ethics training. However, a survey of business ethics concluded that training does not guarantee better ethics. Although awareness and reasoning improve after taking business ethics courses, it is short-lived and soon forgotten. This highlights the need for ongoing and refresher training.

According to London's Institute of Business Ethics, almost one-third of leading British companies now have a written code. Ongoing management training should include the company code of ethics as well as updates on current ethical thinking and practice. Departments should have their own ethical codes and should run ethical training programmes relevant to their functions. Videos should be produced on business ethics and installed in the corporate learning centre.

Posters with the company code of ethics should be put on display on notice boards. Summarised versions of the code should be printed on wallet-sized cards and be issued to all employees for perusal and constant reminding. Periodic reinforcement is important, using methods such as follow-up training, self-study programmes in the corporate learning centre and statements from top management emphasising the importance of ethics.

An annual "ethics audit" is another way of letting employees know the positive effects of their efforts. Managers should be encouraged to review all ethical decisions with their staff, asking,

"What did we do right?" "What did we not do that we should have done?" "What should we do in the future in similar instances?"

Institute of Business Ethics

The Institute of Business Ethics in 1987 recommended that:

- An ethics code should have the support of top management and that employees should be consulted.

- One person should be made responsible for the drafting of the code. That person should consult the company secretary, human resource management and public relations departments.

- *Inter alia*, the code should deal with conflicts of interest, gifts, confidentiality of company information, health and safety, the environment and equal opportunities. The code should state what action will be taken against those who break the code.

- Each employee should get a copy of the code as part of the contract of service. The code should be explained to the employee by their manager.

- The code should be given to shareholders, recruitment agencies and suppliers. Customers should also be told. Some companies print codes or "customer charters" on the back of invoices.

Below is a problem-solving model for resolving ethical issues:

- Select and define the problem, taking into account the company's values and culture. Define the desired outcomes.

- Record the facts surrounding the issue.

- Examine the facts, identify any constraints to resolving the issues and determine how to overcome them.

- Develop alternative solutions and select the best one, having regard to ethical values.

- Identify likely reactions and implement the solution.

- Monitor to see how successful the solution has been and learn from any mistakes made.

This problem-solving approach will help employees to realise the situational nature of ethical problems and analyse and solve them logically.

Legally Required Ethical Standards

There is now a comprehensive regulatory framework with which companies must comply when dealing with most ethical and related issues. If a business doesn't adopt ethics voluntarily, then the government will fill the void with law. Some examples are:

- Employment legislation protecting the rights of workers

- Safety, health and welfare at work legislation

- Pensions

- Data protection legislation protecting employees' rights to privacy and nondisclosure of personal information

- Disclosure of information in company accounts

- Equality legislation

- Maternity protection.

These days also, as part of EU membership, we have to contend with EU directives and the European Social Charter. These directives cover all aspects of business. The European Social Charter covers such areas as the right to training throughout our working lives, information on training, paid educational leave and EU recognition of national vocational qualifications.

The Companies Acts are now based on an EC directive and tighten up previous acts. This was in response to various international financial scandals. These acts have new provisions relating to directors of bankrupt companies and made insider dealing a criminal offence. Directors who act fraudulently can now be held personally liable for company debts. Insider dealing may also allow a third party, who is prejudiced, to sue for damages.

Monitoring Standards — The Professions

The Consultative Committee of Accountancy Bodies (CCAB) has also begun to regulate the format and disclosure of financial information in published annual accounts. These regulations are called Financial Reporting Standards (FRSs) and were previously known as Standard Statements of Accounting Practice (SSAPs).

These are ethical guidelines for accountants when drawing up annual accounts. Although they have only quasi-legal status, they are compulsory for members of the accountancy profession to follow. The various accountancy bodies run training programmes and updates on the FRSs for members. After recent financial scandals, when Chartered Accountants were seen to be helping clients evade tax in offshore accounts, the Irish Government has warned the Institute of Chartered Accountants in Ireland that if the Institute doesn't regulate its own members to the satisfaction of the public then the Government will introduce legislation to do so. It has also indicated that disciplinary action taken against members of the profession should be open and transparent and not done in secret.

Within large companies the role of internal audit departments includes the detection and prevention of fraud and the maintenance of ethics in the financial area. Poor cash and stock control systems can tempt employees to steal. Unregulated purchasing systems can put bribes in the way of employees. Therefore, good ethics and good business practice require that internal controls and internal checks are necessary for the protection of employees and the company. The statutory audit provides a similar function for annual accounts.

Audit committees have been set up in large companies to monitor and evaluate half-yearly and annual financial statements and appraise financial investment on behalf of the Board of Directors. The Cadbury Report on Corporate Governance has made recommendations on the conduct of directors in such areas as disclosure of conflict of interests and insider dealing.

Regulations impose minimum standards. Progressive management should aim to surpass these. Remember, there are still many ethical issues not addressed by law. Hence the need for a company code of ethics.

Where is Ethics Relevant?

Good ethics should be practised by all managers and employees of an organisation. Ethics is necessary in departments such as purchasing, finance, personnel, manufacturing, marketing and research and development. There are ethical issues peculiar to each of these functions that should be addressed.

Already there is substantial literature concerning ethics in accounting — including corporate social reporting, environmental accounting and auditing. For example, the annual report is certainly one key document that reflects an organisation's ethics and ethos.

There are also other ethical issues including corporate social responsibility, illegal payments, mergers, acquisitions, industrial espionage, employee rights and product safety.

Ethics in Human Resource Management

In relation to Human Resource Management we have issues like:

- Privacy
- Appraisals
- Equality
- Nepotism

- Reverse discrimination

- Personality tests

- Electronic eavesdropping

- Industrial relations

- Wages and conditions

- Trade union recognition

- Redundancy

- Dismissal

- Whistle-blowing.

Ethics in General Management

A Harvard Business School survey of 1,200 US readers suggested five aspects of managerial action for business ethics:

- Fair dealing with customers and employees is the most direct way to restore confidence in business morality.

- Steps taken by companies to improve ethical behaviour must come from top management. Poor ethical practices should be discouraged by penalties and good ethical practices should be encouraged by rewards.

- There should be a system for detecting and dealing with violators of the company ethical code.

- Test decisions against what is right rather than what is expedient.

- Don't force others into unethical conduct.

Since the boardroom is the model for the rest of the organisation, it is essential that the best ethics are seen to be adopted there. Training in business ethics at boardroom level should play a role.

The rest of the organisation will take its cue from the ethics or, indeed, lack of ethics, of the boardroom.

Ethics in Marketing

In marketing there are issues like biodegradable packaging, unfair pricing, the giving and receiving of gifts, gratuities and bribes, loss leaders, bait and switch, and cheating customers. Furthermore, in advertising we have persuasion, deception and sexism as in the use of scantily dressed females to sell cars and other merchandise. Sexist advertising is also very prevalent in relation to advertisements promoting drink. The impression is created that you are more virile and sexually appealing if you drink alcohol. The sponsorship of sporting events by tobacco and alcohol companies is seen by many as unethical. There is also the unethical use of psychology such as subliminal advertising and brainwashing. A common case of deception is a person dressed in white in a TV advertisement promoting a product who may give the impression of medical endorsement. The false impression created could be considered unethical.

Marketing situations rank as those causing the most ethical conflict among executives. For example, how can tobacco executives justify ethically the sale of cigarettes when it is now known and medically proven that smoking causes cancer and heart disease and can thus kill? Overall in 1990, tobacco products are estimated to have killed more than 1 million men and about 200,000 women in Europe alone.

Stakeholders and Ethics

The stakeholder theory suggests that we practise good ethics in our dealing with customers, suppliers, lenders, shareholders, central and local government, employees, managers, the local community and trade unions. The stakeholder theory is shown below:

Stakeholder Theory

Customers expect fair dealing, value for money, quality, honest and truthful advertising and good after-sales service. Also, media concern over the unknown long-term health implications of genetically modified food has alarmed customers who question the motives of companies producing such foodstuffs. Are they more interested in making profits than the health, safety and welfare of customers? Suppliers expect continuous business, fair dealing and to be paid on time. Some businesses maintain their cash liquidity at the expense of suppliers by taking very long credit periods. Surely this is morally wrong and unethical? Are managers aware of the ethics involved?

Lenders expect the repayment of loans and interest payments when due. Shareholders want to be kept informed, achieve capital growth for their investment and dividend payments when due. They also expect directors to manage the company in an ethical manner with the shareholder's interest in mind.

The central government expects businesses to obey the law, pay their taxes and provide employment opportunities. Local government demands compliance with by-laws and respect for the environment and the rights of local communities.

The local community expects corporate responsibility and support for local athletic, charity, cultural and social activities. It expects companies not to endanger local communities by environmental pollution such as fumes, toxic waste, emissions and noise. Some companies have a policy of encouraging their managers to get involved in community affairs. Corporate social responsibility is good public relations and good business.

Employees expect security of employment, fair pay, good working conditions, training and development opportunities, equity of treatment, job satisfaction and reasonable prospects. In the unfortunate case of company closure, they expect fair redundancy payments and job counselling. Managers expect security of employment, power, achievement and career advancement. Unions expect recognition, fair wages and conditions of employment for employees, right to collective bargaining, employee share option schemes and participation in decision making for members.

Lewis (1985) summaries the conclusions of previous research done on business ethics as follows:

- Sound ethics is good for business.

- Profit should not be the sole motive for business.

- Middle and lower managers feel more keenly the pressures to compromise personal standards.

- Competition can cause people to ignore ethical considerations.

- People with a strong, well-defined personal code are most likely to act ethically.

- Ethics tends to be highest with the youngest employees. It is also highest with those in the final decade of their careers.

- Pressure from superiors to achieve results can cause unethical behaviour.

- Managers and employees who are very loyal and identify closely with their companies can rationalise unethical practice and not feel personally responsible.

So in modern business there are all sorts of pressures on managers to adopt unethical practices. An individuals capacity to rationalise unethical actions on the grounds of expediency or pragmatism is unlimited and it is often surprising who will become involved in questionable behaviour. When faced with an ethical dilemma, executives tend to opt for the profitable course of action rather than the ethical one. A code of ethics helps to counteract this and maintain high standards of ethical behaviour.

Summary

We need ethical standards to live by as individuals and organisations. Without these we are unlikely to make a success of our personal or business lives. Many a political and business career has been ruined by an abuse of ethics. Indeed, many a corporation's image has been damaged and some have even been put out of business through poor ethical practices.

Organisations which fail to abide by normal standards of ethical behaviour will have it thrust upon them by legislation. Most large organisations have now drawn up codes of ethics for their business. The practice of good ethics is good for people and good for business.

Ethics are monitored by the law, professions, the media and environmental groups. Many of these have drawn up their own code of ethics.

Chapter 6 Mind Map

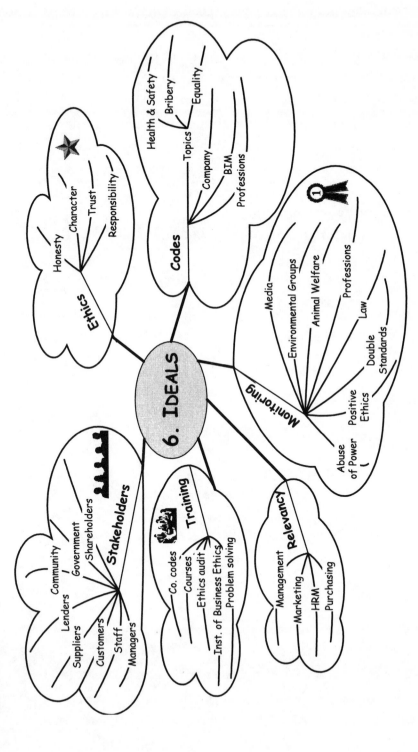

7. Belief

◆ *What is the self-fulfilling prophecy?*

◆ *What are self-limiting beliefs?*

◆ *What are the Placebo and Voodoo effects?*

◆ *How are the mind and body interlinked?*

◆ *What is the SAVER model?*

◆ *What are the beliefs for business success?*

The Self-fulfilling Prophecy

People move in the direction of their dominant thoughts. You become what you expect to become and you achieve what you expect to achieve. You see what you believe. People's perception of reality is not reality itself. We tend to find what we look for in people or situations: good or evil, problems or solutions, opportunities or threats.

If we have low expectations for ourselves we will never achieve much. What the mind can conceive and believe it may achieve. You are limited to a large extent by your own expectations, beliefs and fears. Expect the best and the best will happen: convert problems into opportunities and see the positive side to life's trials and tribulations. Everybody has problems. Nobody escapes the normal ups and downs of life. Don't expect to be happy all the time. You must be able to live with the bad days as well as the good. Become solution-centred rather than problem-centred. See the best in people rather than the worst.

Life is a self-fulfilling prophecy. Elvis Presley, the King of Rock and Roll, died aged 42 years shortly before his 43rd birthday. By a strange coincidence, he died at exactly the same age, and due to the same apparent cause, as his mother to whom he was very devoted. The official inquest suggested that his death was due to a heart attack contributed to by drug overdose, but was it a case of the self-fulfilling prophecy in action?

In our quest for personal excellence we are influenced by the expectations of others and by the expectations of ourselves. The Pygmalion Effect suggests that, in addition to our own expectations, we live up to the expectations of others. In experiments, students were found to live up to the high expectations set by their teachers. If our managers set high standards we are often motivated to achieve them. Managers can draw out the best from their staff by leading by example, treating them as intelligent, resourceful and empowered human beings. On the other hand, they can draw out the worst in people by setting a bad example and treating them as lacking in intelligence, ideas and initiative.

Fear

Most of our worst fears are never realised. We worry about things that may happen in the future, but in practice 99 per cent of our worries never materialise. It is soon enough to worry about things when they happen. Fear has been defined as **F**alse **E**vidence **A**ppearing **R**eal. Fear of failure, fear of success, fear of the unknown, fear of change and fear of what other people will think are some of the common fears confronting us. Fear can prevent us from undertaking new challenges and exploring the unknown. Fear is a natural condition and can be channelled positively. It provides us with adrenaline which gives us energy to confront potential dangers. It is only uncontrolled fear which is a problem. As Rudyard Kipling said: "Courage is not the absence of fear, it is the control of fear."

Fear of success is one of the greatest deterrents to high performance. Fear often brings out the wrath and envy of others which is not a pleasant experience for the successful person who becomes the target of such outbursts. The continuing burden of meeting the expectations of others also contributes to the fear of success syndrome.

Disempowering Beliefs

Whatever you believe with feeling becomes your reality. Beliefs can be empowering or self-limiting. Sometimes barriers are traditional and psychological rather than real. Your limitations are all in your head. Common disempowering beliefs include:

- I feel uneasy in social occasions
- I can't draw a straight line
- I'm tone deaf
- I could never speak in public
- I'm a bit of a loner
- I can't remember names
- I'm useless at maths

- I'm a slow reader

- I'm not mechanically-minded

- I'm never on time

- I haven't enough time

- How could I be so stupid?

- It happens to me every time

- I can't get anything right

- This is going to be very difficult

- This is going to be another one of those days

- I wouldn't be able for that promotion

- The jobs are filled before they are advertised

- Nepotism is rife in job selection

- I'm not earning enough to save

- I'll save someday but not now.

Empowering Beliefs

The problem with disempowering beliefs is that they tend to become self-fulfilling prophecies. The theory of multiple intelligence suggests that we have the basic ability to do almost anything we want provided we have the self-belief and make the commitment. Empowering beliefs include:

- Everything happens for a purpose. Disappointments are a natural part of life. Try to see the positive aspects of even tragic events in your life.

- We can do anything we want to do, if it interests us enough. If we don't know how to do something we can learn.

- Look at setbacks as stepping stones to success. There is no such thing as failure, only results. Learn from the feedback. Life is a cycle of continuous improvement.

- Whatever happens, take responsibility for your own actions. Avoid the blame culture.

- People are your greatest resource. Exploit this resource by tapping into the natural creativity and ingenuity of people around you. Don't be afraid to ask questions.

- Realise that you can't change the world, but you can change yourself.

- Work is play. If your work is your hobby and your hobby is your work then you can say that you are truly successful.

- Prosperity is a state of mind and is a relative concept. Some people with very little and a positive attitude are more prosperous than others who are very wealthy but disillusioned.

- There is no success without commitment and hard work. Getting ahead in your management career is not going to be easy. Are you willing to pay the price?

Dream the Impossible Dream

For many years it was thought impossible to run a mile faster than four minutes. Then Roger Bannister came along and the psychological barrier was broken in addition to a world record being created. Numerous runners subsequently broke the barrier and new records are now continually being set. Split seconds can make the difference between world champions and also-rans. It is that little extra effort, belief and commitment that give the competitive edge. If you use only about 1 per cent of your brain's capacity, as some psychologists believe, then by just using another 1 per cent you could double your potential capacity for wealth and success.

Pilot Chuck Yeager broke the sound barrier on 14 October 1947. At that time, backed by scientific evidence, eminent scientists believed that the barrier was impenetrable. Chuck was warned he would not survive the attempt but would disintegrate in the process. Supersonic flight is now commonplace and the myth of the impenetrable barrier and disintegration has been put to rest.

Ignorance is often bliss. Aerodynamic scientific research shows that the bumblebee, because of its body weight in relation to its wing size, can't fly. However, the bumblebee is unaware of this scientific facts and flies regardless. Many people thought space travel a fantasy but it is now fast becoming a reality.

Reflect on the following inspirational poem which highlights the importance of self-belief and positive thinking:

If you think you are beaten, you are;
If you think you dare not, you don't;
If you'd like to win, but think you can't,
It's almost a cinch you won't.

If you think you'll lose, you're lost,
For out in the world we find
Success begins with a fellow's WILL;
It's all in the state of mind

If you think you're outclassed, you are;
You've got to think high to rise.
You've just got to be sure of yourself
Before you can win the prize.

Life's battles don't always go
To the stronger or faster man,
But sooner or later the man who wins
Is the man who THINKS he can.

Author unknown.

The Placebo & Voodoo Effects

In medicine there is a well-known phenomenon known as the *placebo effect*. It is a question of faith conquering all. People who have intense faith in their doctors and believe that they will get well, irrespective of the medicine taken (it may be just plain water), often amaze their physicians and friends with their unexpected recovery. It seems to be a case of mind over matter. Faith healing, which customarily involves touching, is based on trust and belief and often produces "miracle" cures. These cures may be the result of the placebo effect.

The power of belief can also be a negative force. In the Voodoo religion a curse from a witch doctor may prove fatal for the victim. Members of the tribe who have a death spell cast upon them die within a few days. The power of sincerely-held beliefs, negative thinking and pre-set mindsets is immense. Having a scarcity as opposed to an abundance mentality is also linked with negative thinking, particularly fears based upon beliefs that there is insufficient money, talent and love to go around. Such beliefs often give rise to envy, fear and jealousy. Contrary to popular opinion new competition often stimulates greater demand and more prosperity for all.

Negative thoughts, feelings and attitudes can cause depression, anxiety, out of control feelings, stress and emotional distress. Emotionally distressed people are inclined to worry, argue, make mistakes, have accidents and have high rates of absenteeism. Worry is a rocking chair that gives you something to do but never gets you anywhere. Control your thoughts and control your behaviour by accentuating the positive and eliminating the negative.

The Mind and Body are One System

The mind and body are integrated. They are part of the one system. What the mind dwells upon the body acts upon. Change your body and change your mind. Change your mind and change your body.

Change your thinking, attitudes and beliefs and change your life. Nothing in life has any meaning except the meaning you give it. By choosing your thoughts, you can create either hell or heaven on earth. By choosing your thoughts carefully you can control your life. Thoughts come before every action. People feel good about themselves to the extent that they are in control of their thoughts and consequently their actions. Positive thoughts attract positive events. Positive people attract like-minded friends and so you have a positive reinforcing cycle.

Doctors now recognise that many ailments and diseases are caused by stress. Sixty to seventy per cent of visitors to doctors' surgeries are sick because of emotional problems. For example, ulcers are often not caused by what we eat but what is eating us. Your body believes every word you think and say. So make sure you're thinking positive thoughts. Cancer and other diseases are often triggered by high levels of individual stress which in turn is fuelled by negative thoughts.

The SAVER Model

The mind thinks in three dimensions, as shown through the mnemonic PEW:

- **P**ictures
- **E**motions
- **W**ords.

Psychologists have found that the impact affirmations have on our subconscious can be broken down as follows:

- Reading — 10 per cent
- Reading and visualisation — 55 per cent
- Reading, visualisation and feeling — 100 per cent.

This is why, in addition to reciting affirmations, you should visualise and emotionalise their content. All meaningful and lasting change begins in our imagination as thoughts and then works its way into reality. Affirmations are the mechanism through which this can be achieved. It is significant that Albert Einstein's approach to learning emphasised using and integrating all of the senses. Use the SAVER mnemonic as a tool to programme your mind for success.

Substitute positive for negative thoughts. Two men looked out of prison bars; one saw mud and the other saw stars. Reframe past negative situations so as to see them in a more positive light. See them from different points of view; your own, another person's and a detached point of view. Positive thinkers have high self-esteem. Positive and happy people produce a high level of endorphins. Cortisol is one of the hormones released by the adrenal glands in response to stress. This hormone is toxic to the brain and high levels kill off millions of brain cells. A stressful life can damage your brain as well as your body. Some doctors believe that cortisol toxicity is one of the primary causes of Alzheimer's disease. So manage your stress to help keep your brain in top learning form.

Endorphins also strengthen your immune system. In other words, endorphins improve your resistance to disease. Positive and happy people produce a high level of endorphins. Laughter is the best medicine as it produces high levels of endorphins. On the other hand, the level of endorphins falls in angry and stressed people. So being happy and developing a positive attitude to life is good for your health, wealth and success. A happy person is not a person in a certain set of circumstances but rather a person with a certain set of attitudes. Happiness is a state of mind.

Affirm. Programme your mind with affirmations. Affirmations should be positive (state what you want rather than what you don't want), personal and made in the present tense. The wording of affirmations should be clear, concise and specific. Use constructive self-talk like "I want to"; "I can", "I look forward to"; "I'll do it" and "I'll be successful". By controlling your self-talk, you can control your life. The best time of the day to do your affirmations is when you're relaxed or first thing in the morning or last thing before you fall asleep at might. Some examples of affirmations which might be worth taking on board include:

Learning Affirmations

- I believe in lifelong learning

- I am committed to unconscious competence

- I am able to focus my concentration when I want to

- My mental capacity and efficiency is improving daily

- I am able to remember what I want to remember

- I feed and stimulate my mind with new learning opportunities

- I am able to relax and increase my recall

- Every day in every way my memory is improving

- Learning is something I thoroughly enjoy

- Learning, remembering and concentrating are easy for me

- I believe reading is important to my self-development

- My mind moves efficiently and effectively

- I'm a genius.

Personal Success Affirmations

- I always act from personal integrity and a high standard of ethics.

- I am committed to doing everything it takes to be successful in life

- I'm confident of success

- If it's going to be, it's up to me

- I like myself

- I believe something wonderful is going to happen to me today

- This is the day that the Lord has made, I will rejoice and be glad in it

- I can do it

- Now I'm achieving my goals

- I am supremely calm

- My self-talk is positive

- I think, speak and act with great enthusiasm

- I'm an action person, I do first things first and one thing at a time

- I choose my own goals, otherwise other people will choose them for me

- I will achieve my goals and take every setback as purely temporary

- I develop feelings of self-respect and esteem in others

- I gain great benefit from reciting my affirmations at least twice every day.

Interpersonal Relations Affirmations

- I hugely enjoy meeting new people.

- I have a confident friendly smile.

- I like people and they like me.

- People respect me and listen to my ideas

- I stand and carry myself in a confident and friendly manner.

- I believe most people are sincere and honest.

Visualise successful situations. Affirmations should be used in conjunction with visualisation. Visualisations should be frequent, intense, vivid and durable. For example, "If things are to happen, then I must make them happen". If you practise and do it right in your imagination you'll do it right in life. Programme your mind for success. See yourself achieving your desired outcomes. See yourself successfully practising that new skill. Experience the intense emotions. See yourself in that graduation photograph complete with gown and mortarboard. See yourself working toward and eventually accepting that long-wished-for promotion. Hold those pictures in your mind's eye and replay them frequently. Make continuous self-improvement and lifelong learning your goal.

Emotionalise. Imprint your feelings and thoughts by imagining how you will feel, see, hear and experience success. Imagine the graduation ceremony with all the sights and sounds and the reception afterwards. See yourself being congratulated by your family and friends. Feel the strength of the handshake. Experience the sense of pride. Enjoy the well-earned adulation and recognition. Emotional involvement will imprint the scene on your imagination.

Rehearse. Sports psychologists place heavy emphasis on motivation through mental training and positive reinforcement for the athletes they coach. They have found that mental rehearsal is nearly as good as doing it in practice. They believe in the power of the mind. Great golfers, tennis players, boxers and runners practise winning in their imagination as well as physical practice. Airline pilots go through simulation training using practised physical movements and mental rehearsal before they actually fly. The astronauts who went to the moon spent years in simulated training in the desert and elsewhere in the physical conditions they expected to find on the moon. The experience of weightlessness was achieved by training underwater. Planning and continuous physical and mental rehearsal imprinted the appropriate actions until they became habitual responses. This created the appropriate mindsets that paved the way for their success. Remember, the subconscious mind is unable to tell the difference between actual experience and one that is vividly imagined. Subjective thought becomes objective reality. Mentally rehearsing ensures successful outcomes.

Beliefs for Better Business Performance

Customer Orientation

The customer is king. The traditional view of customers as an appendage to an organisation is no longer acceptable. Customers are not only external people who buy your goods and services but also internal people within the company. In this definition, everyone is a customer. Internal customers are simply the next process, or where the work goes next. The customer orientation viewpoint should permeate the whole organisation. For example, a supervisor's customers are their employees and their manager, in addition to others who may call on their services for help or advice. All customers are important. Internal customers should get the same quality service as external customers now expect. If you don't look after your employees, don't be surprised if they do likewise and fail to look after their customers.

Zero Defects and Getting It Right First Time

If everybody tried their utmost to produce quality work then the number of rejects, mistakes, corrections and adjustments would be reduced significantly. The need for controls, checks and inspections would also be reduced. Make people responsible for the quality of their own work. Controls create the mental attitude that the system will pick it up anyway, so why care? Thus too many controls show a lack of trust, create a dependence mentality, stifle initiative and thus can be counterproductive.

Total Quality Management (TQM)

TQM aims to eliminate all waste and at the same time satisfy customer needs. As we saw above, customers include internal as well as external customers which means that everybody in the organisation has a supplier and a customer. Therefore, everybody tries to ensure that their output is correct when it leaves them, and that they meet their customers' needs. In a TQM environment employees are dedicated to continuous improvement. They work in teams to solve problems and increase efficiencies.

Continuous Improvement

There is always a better way to do anything. New technology, different perspectives and improved methods always offer scope for improvements. The Taylorite view of the one best way is no longer accepted. An environment to encourage continuous improvement should be created in the workplace. Creativity should be facilitated through quality circles, suggestion schemes, incentive programmes and brainstorming sessions. Use the untapped creative potential and hidden expertise of your workforce.

Lifelong Learning

Your employees are your greatest resource. Employees should be encouraged to learn on the job and off the job. Educational support schemes should be put in place to encourage people to undertake formal studies at certificate, diploma and degree level. Postgraduate studies should be supported for junior, middle and senior management. Individual training plans should be put in place to identify training and development needs. A corporate learning centre should be established in the workplace as a visible sign of management support for lifelong learning. In the future, knowledge and creativity will be the most important competitive edge.

Learning Organisation

A learning organisation is one that encourages learning at all levels. Every individual in the organisation is encouraged to be better tomorrow than they are today. The organisation is totally committed to continuous improvement of every part of its operations including its products, services, systems, procedures, teamwork and organisation. As the learning organisation develops, employee morale will be enhanced and the service to customers transformed. An organisation needs to be able to adapt to change. It also needs to be able to anticipate change. The latter needs futuristic thinking, creativity and innovation. A learning organisation has the following beliefs:

- Learning is fun

- A win-win attitude in negotiations

- Lifelong learning is what success is all about

- A questioning approach to all aspects of the business is needed to improve

- Open communication between management and staff is the norm including open-book management

- Focus on customers

- A culture of learning from mistakes.

The following are some of the programmes necessary to develop a learning organisation:

- Suggestion schemes

- Quality circles

- Good reward systems

- Management by wandering about (MBWA)

- Teamwork

- Job rotation, job enrichment and job enlargement

- Multiskilling and a flexible workforce

- Educational support schemes

- Training and development

- Corporate learning centres

- Decentralised structures and delegation.

The importance of intellectual property rights is now recognised on the company balance sheet as assets. Trademarks, patents and brands are common examples.

Empowerment

Empowerment is about giving employees control and responsibility over their own work. It is a new psychological contract where opportunities for job satisfaction and fulfilment are provided in exchange for a worker's loyalty and commitment. It is the philosophy that everyone in the organisation should feel a sense of ownership and pride. To do this you must give employees power to make decisions concerning their own work. To make effective decisions employees need access to information and resources.

Some organisations practise open-book management. This means making financial information freely available to employees and explaining to them its significance. This helps employees to see how they can control or reduce costs and improve product quality. Dr J.M. Juran, one of the gurus of quality management, insisted that quality must be the responsibility of each employee through self-supervision.

In autonomous maintenance, operators are given the right to do basic maintenance on their own machines. The operators are closest to the machines so they can monitor their usage and maintain them accordingly. Some organisations are now encouraging employees to identify their own training needs and draw up their own individual training plans. These are then agreed with their supervisors. Teamwork, autonomous work groups, cellular manufacturing processes, quality circles, job rotation and multiskilling are all ways of empowering the workforce.

People Are Your Most Important Resource

People have an intrinsic need for psychological growth. Therefore, organisation structures and practices that limit opportunities for personal growth are harmful to the individual and ultimately to the organisation. Training and development is an investment rather than an expense. Unlike fixed assets, your human resources will appreciate over time. The costs of training will be recovered many times over by the increased efficiency and effectiveness of the workforce. Morale, job satisfaction and productivity will improve.

Integrated Nature of Beliefs and Learning

The environment, behaviour, capability, beliefs, identity and spirituality are all interlinked and determine the effectiveness and success of your life.

The Environment

This is where you work and the people you work with. Some people attribute their success to being in the right place at the right time. In other words, they are saying that the environment was the reason for their success. If you work in a challenging work environment with intelligent professionally qualified people then you can only grow and develop.

Some companies have very good educational support schemes and actively encourage their staff to pursue academic studies appropriate to their own self-development and to the needs of the organisation. They also actively encourage their staff to attend training and development programmes. They encourage their staff to organise themselves into learning sets. Such an environment will stimulate and challenge the minds of your staff and develop them as people and have a positive effect on the company's bottom line.

Behaviour

This is the level of our specific actions. It includes thoughts as well as actions since thoughts are the progenitors of actions. This quote by Frank Outlaw captures its essence:

> Watch your thoughts; they become words.
> Watch your words; they become actions.
> Watch your actions; they become habits.
> Watch your habits; they become character.
> Watch your character; it becomes your destiny.

What we do is not random. Our behaviour achieves a purpose. However, this may not always be clear to us. If what you are doing at the moment is not achieving your goals then you need to do something different. Change your behaviour and change your results. Behaviour can become habitual and therefore very difficult to change. Habits are a pattern of activity which, through repetition, have become automatic. Habits are controlled by the subconscious. It took a long time for them to be imprinted on the subconscious and therefore it's going to take some time and effort to remove or change them. Nevertheless, all behaviour can be changed if you know the right process.

The SAVER model discussed earlier can be used to change behaviour patterns. To succeed in your career you may have to change your current behaviour, particularly if your current behaviour is not helping you progress towards your goals. Many people are in a rut, and blame and complain without really doing anything about it. It is a very simple truth that you must take action if you want to change the direction of your life. Different actions produce different results. Learning is but a change in behaviour.

Capability

This is behaviour which we have practised so often that it has become a skill. It has become an automatic process. We can do these actions without really thinking about them and often do other things concurrently. It is at the level of unconscious competence. Capability includes thinking strategies and manual skills. We walk and talk and take very little notice of just what sophisticated and marvellous skills these mundane actions are. Our driving skills are an automatic reflex action. We have learnt the basics of reading, writing and arithmetic and can exercise the skills with great proficiency. We may be good at sport or playing a musical instrument.

It takes many years before our capability or skill in a particular area is fully developed. So don't expect to become an expert overnight! For example, despite the improvement in user-friendly software, it still takes training and many months of practice to become proficient in PC skills. It usually takes up to ten years to become an expert in any field. Our capabilities play an important role in our success.

Beliefs and Values

This is what we believe is true and what is important to us. Beliefs and values are our guiding principles. Beliefs determine our behaviour. They act as permissions and prohibitions. The sources of our beliefs are our upbringing, peer influence, modelling, past traumas and repetitive experiences. Are there skills you would like to develop but believe that you cannot? Many people believe that they are not mathematically minded and, therefore, shy away from any subject with a mathematical content. Naturally they will never develop their mathematical abilities. It's the self-fulfilling prophecy in action again! We are also capable of holding conflicting beliefs and values. We say one thing and do another.

Identity

Have you ever heard anyone say: "I'm just not that type of person." "I can never see myself in that role." They can never see themselves as public speakers and, therefore, they are likely never to become public speakers. They can never see themselves as managers and therefore they are unlikely to become managers. This is an identity statement. Your identity is a sense of who you are and what you stand for. Identity determines your mission in life. However, you can build, shape and change your identity if you desire to do so.

Spirituality

This is your connection to yourself, others, nature and to the universe. Rapport at this level is a spiritual sense of being one with humankind, the universe and a higher power. You came out of the earth; you are nurtured by the earth and you will return to the earth. We are part of a continuous ecological cycle.

Summary

The self-fulfilling prophecy and the Pygmalion effect were discussed. We become what we think about all day long. Our beliefs, values and attitudes determine what we become. We need to substitute empowering for disempowering beliefs. The Placebo effect is a question of mind over body. The mind and body are interlinked. The Voodoo effect can kill.

The SAVER model to programme your mind for success was highlighted. SAVER stands for:

- Substitute positive for negative thoughts

- Affirm

- Visualise

- Emotionalise

- Rehearse.

The core beliefs for business success were explored. These are:

- Customer orientation

- Total quality management

- Zero defects and getting it right first time

- Continuous improvement

- Lifelong learning

- The learning organisation

- Empowerment

- People are your most important resource.

The environment, behaviour, capability, beliefs, identify and spirituality are all interlinked and determine the effectiveness and success of your life.

Chapter 7 Mind Map

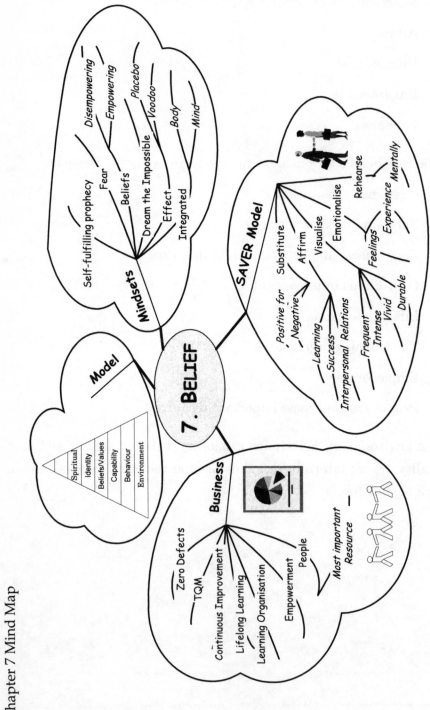

8. Enthusiasm

"One man has enthusiasm for 30 minutes, another for 30 days, but it is the man who has it for 30 years who makes a success of his life" — Edward B. Butler

"Enthusiasm is everything. It must be taut and vibrating like a guitar string." — Pele

---

- ♦ *How can you create passion for your work?*

- ♦ *What is the optimum experience model?*

- ♦ *What is faith?*

- ♦ *What is the PACE model?*

- ♦ *How can you create enthusiasm in your life?*

- ♦ *How can you motivate yourself and others?*

- ♦ *What is the DREAM model of learning?*

Passion

Do what you love and love what you do. Doing what you love is the key to fulfilment. Do you hate Monday mornings? If you do, then it is very likely that you're in the wrong job. You should look forward to your work with eager anticipation. You are unlikely to be inspired or excited by work which you find monotonous and routine. Yet how many of us are stuck in a rut in dead-end jobs that no longer interest us? Formal organisations can stifle our initiative and kill off our dreams and ambitions.

What is worth doing, is worth doing well. So if you find your job uninteresting, you are unlikely to give it your best shot. Successful people have a passion for their work. If they weren't being paid to do it they would probably do it anyway. Their work is their life. Their work is like their hobby. Asked for the secret of success, one executive who had worked his way up through the ranks said: "It's simple. I never had a job I didn't like."

Many people spend their lives climbing a ladder and get to the top before realising its leaning against the wrong wall. They may have attained all the material success in the world but at what cost to themselves in terms of job satisfaction, health, relationships and a balanced purposeful life. They end up alone, with no true friends and a broken marriage.

Enthusiastic people are grateful for what they have — their unique qualities. They think of what they have and of what they can give. They realise that comparisons with others can be counter-productive and so they just try and improve their own standards by trying to be better all the time. They have a natural curiosity and have a childlike wonder for life.

Enthusiasm of others cannot be bought. You must earn it by example and sensitivity. As Clarence Francis said:

> You can buy people's time; you can buy their physical presence at a given place; you can even buy a measured number of their skilled muscular motions per hour. But you cannot buy enthusiasm . . . you cannot buy loyalty . . . you cannot buy the devotion of hearts, minds, or souls. You must earn these.

Optimum Experience Model

The model below is based on work by the psychologist Mihaly Csikszentmihalyi, who was interested in discovering when people undergo optimal experiences.

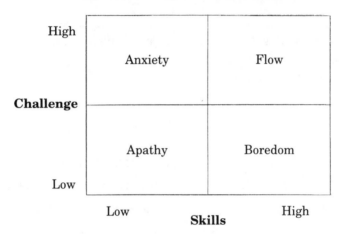

Optimum Experience Model

Source: Csikszentmihalyi (1991)

Work activities that offer a high challenge and use a low level of skills create anxiety. Work activities which offer a low level of challenge and use a low level of skills create apathy. Work activities which offer a high challenge and use a high level of skills create flow or optimum work satisfaction. This is the ideal situation. Work activities that offer a lower level of challenge than your high level of skills create boredom.

Looking at work in terms of skills you have and the level required to do the work can help you to examine which parts of your work life may be sources of job dissatisfaction.

Your attitude to work will also be a factor in whether or not you experience job satisfaction. It is important to practise positive affirmations in relation to work. Notice the different effects the following self-talk is likely to have:

Positive Self-Talk	Negative Self-talk
"This is a real challenge."	"This work is too difficult."
"If I practise good time management I'm sure I'll get it done on time."	"I'll never get this done on time."
"This looks quite difficult but I'm sure I'll be able to figure it out or get help."	"I can't do this."
"Nothing is impossible. It's just a question of self-belief, focused concentration and application."	"This is impossible."

Faith

Faith is a belief in your own capabilities, your dreams and the providence of God. Faith is belief without evidence — belief that you can achieve a goal without knowing exactly how you're going to do it. None of the great achievements and inventions in history would have been achieved without faith. Faith provides the vision, hope, commitment and driving force for the future. Hope in the form of a positive outlook is what keeps most of us going from day to day. We believe tomorrow is another day and that the best is yet to come.

Faith is the engine which drives your enthusiasm. Faith drives you forward to the realisation of your purpose. People with faith provide exemplary service to others. People with faith are grateful for what they have and believe in sharing it with others. People without faith often suffer from psychological problems. Carl Jung once said: "In about one-third of my cases, the patients are suffering from no clinically definable neurosis, but from the senselessness and emptiness of their lives".

Your mind believes, conceives and does what it is consistently told. Having faith consists of sending strong appropriate affirmations and visualisations repeatedly to the unconscious mind. This sets up the unconscious mind to act out the instructions as it can't tell the difference between a real experience and one that is vividly imagined.

A modern example of tremendous faith and devotion to the service of others was the late Mother Teresa. Her commitment to and unselfish work with the poor and outcasts of Calcutta brought her worldwide admiration and respect from all irrespective of religious belief. Faith, hope and charity were the driving forces in her life. Her total faith in God inspired her to found an organisation, the Missionaries of Charity, which now helps the poor and rejected in 123 countries throughout the world. This faith was reinforced by her hope in the expectation of salvation and the beatific vision in Heaven and her belief in the tenet, "Love God and thy neighbour as thyself." Mother Teresa said: "Yesterday is gone and tomorrow has not yet come, so we must live each day as if it were our last so that when God calls us we are ready, and prepared to die with a clean heart."

Keeping Things in Perspective

If we ignore our spiritual needs, we will lack a sense of purpose in life and not know why we are in this world. We may live our lives as if we were immortal. We may ignore the fact that life and death are interconnected and that some day we may be called upon to account for our actions. From the moment we are born we are in fact slowly dying. Always keeping in mind that some day you will exit from this life should give you a sense of perspective on life and help you to prioritise the really important issues.

Most people these days are caught up so much with the chores of living that they spend no time thinking about the meaning and purpose of life.

> For what shall it profit a man if he shall gain the whole world, and lose his own soul? Or what shall a man give in exchange for his soul? (Mark 8: 36–7)

Few give any thought to the following fundamental questions which form the mystery of life:

- What is the purpose of my life?

- What is there after this life?

- Who am I?

- Where have I come from?

- Why have I been put on earth?

- Why is there evil in the world?

- What do I contribute to society?

- Where am I going?

Socrates advised "Know thyself." His famous student Plato said: "The life which is unexamined is not worth living."

The PACE Model

Many of us haven't the confidence to come to grips with the consequences surrounding the mortality of our own lives and ignore our spiritual needs. The mnemonic PACE will help you focus on the important issues of life:

- **Perspective.** This is the ability to recognise the important things in life and to live accordingly. Having a mission, vision and purpose will give direction and meaning to your life. Balance your life so that in addition to your work you spend sufficient time with your family and friends and with yourself. Real success is peace of mind and being surrounded by friends and a loving family.

- **Autonomy.** This is the feeling that you are control of your life, that you are responsible and that you are not being manipulated by others. Live your life on your own terms and in line with your conscience and sense of self-worth. It is not necessary to demean yourself by sycophantic behaviour to progress in your career.

- **Connectedness.** This is the positive relationship you need to build with yourself, family, friends and co-workers and the spiritual connection with nature and with God.

- **Exercise.** You need to exercise your body and mind in order to maintain your health. Health is your wealth! Many of the health problems of modern life have been contributed to or caused by our sedentary lifestyle, fast pace of life, fast food diets, alcohol consumption and smoking. Without health life has little value. Many a rich person would give away all their worldly wealth in return for even a few months of health.

Motivation

Enthusiastic people are mostly motivated by moving towards the achievement of positive and attractive goals rather than the need to avoid pain or punishment. They like challenge and responsibility and take pride in their work. However, there are many sources of motivation. Motivation is determined by multiple needs including the need for money to pay for basic living requirements. However, once these basic needs are met the other needs take over and gain importance.

People are motivated by different things. What motivates one person may not motivate another. The belief that there is a prime source of motivation is an oversimplification. The more common sources of motivation can be recalled by the mnemonic PURE SCRIBES:

- **Power.** Some people are driven by the need for power. They want power over other people and resources. Politicians are often driven by the need for power and prestige.

- **Urge to win.** The need to win, to be first, is a great motivator. Hence competitions, medals and football finals. The World Cup is driven by the need to win. People circumnavigate the globe in a canoe because it has never been done before. They dream the impossible dream. Yesterday's dreams are the necessities of today; today's dreams are the opportunities of tomorrow.

- **Recognition.** The pride and status involved if the outcome is achieved. The admiration of colleagues and friends. As a manager don't be afraid to praise your staff for work well done. Most people get little recognition or praise in their lives. Your staff will revel in the praise.

- **Emotional security.** The friendship, affection and acceptance of being emotionally involved with someone. This is the reason why many people get married.

- **Self-esteem.** This is feeling good about yourself. It naturally follows the achievement of some desirable goal. Long-service awards, titles, pens, badges, and medals are all examples of awards that companies make to meet the ego needs of staff.

- **Creativity.** There seems to be a natural hunger in human beings to pursue challenges by seeking out the unusual, solve problems, innovate and exploit your talents to the best of your ability. Maslow calls this the need for self-actualisation.

- **Respect.** Becoming prominent in your profession or career may win you the respect and admiration of your peers. This can be a driving motivator for many.

- **Interest.** Without enthusiasm and an inherent interest in the topic there is unlikely to be lasting motivation. Interest alone can take you very far. This is the core of job satisfaction. People who love their work have no problems of energy and commitment. Job enrichment, job enlargement, job rotation, team-based structures and empowerment can all help to make work more interesting and fulfilling.

- **Belonging.** This is the need for affectionate relations with others and a sense of belonging to a group. Many people will put up with an uninteresting job if the people they work with are friendly, supportive and interesting. In managers the need for power and achievement takes priority over the need for affiliation. When it comes to the crunch, ambitious managers are often prepared to sacrifice friendship in the pursuit of power.

- **Equity.** This is the ratio of rewards to effort. What other people get for similar effort is used as a benchmark to see if the reward to effort ratio is fair. A perceived inequity creates tension which motivates a person to rectify the situation. Many industrial relations disputes are triggered by changing long-standing relativities between groups. If these are disturbed it is seen as unfair and may result in bitter and prolonged industrial relations disputes.

Enthusiasm for Learning

Just like any other area of life, to be successful in learning you need plenty of enthusiasm. The DREAM model will help you realise that dream:

- **Desire.** You must really want to learn. Desire comes from an enthusiasm for the subject and an ambition to become an expert in the particular field.

- **Relevancy.** The learning must be relevant to your present needs. For example, if you work as a middle manager, an MBA or professional qualification would be most relevant to your current and future career prospects. You would also be able to see application for the knowledge learnt on a day-to-day basis in the work situation. Application reinforces the knowledge and makes the learning more meaningful.

- **Expectation.** You must have high expectations of success. Believe and you shall achieve. The self-belief must be matched by hard work and dedication to learning.

- **Anticipation.** Anticipate in your mind's eye the feelings you will experience when you are successful. Constantly keep this in front of you. Imagine the pride you will feel and the respect you will gain from work colleagues when you eventually achieve that MBA!

- **Motivation.** There are two types of motivation — towards and away-from. Towards motivation is the best. Here you are motivated by the prospect of achieving the MBA and the success in your career that this achievement is likely to bring you. Away-from motivation can also be useful. This is the pain of rejection and lack of progress that you are likely to encounter in your career if you don't get that MBA! Obviously, a combination of towards and away-from motivation brings the best of both worlds.

Summary

Enthusiasm is a passion for what you do. Without enthusiasm there is little chance of true success. A model was explored to show how optimum experiences can be achieved.

Faith is the engine which drives enthusiasm. The three basic tenets of faith, hope and charity will help you live a more fulfilling life.

A prescriptive mnemonic called PACE for good living was suggested:

- Perspective

- Autonomy

- Connectedness

- Exercise.

Motivation and enthusiasm are interlinked. Without one the other is largely ineffective. The sources of motivation are multiple. The more common sources can be recalled by the mnemonic PURE SCRIBES:

- Power

- Urge to win

- Recognition

- Emotional security

- Self-esteem

- Creativity

- Respect

- Interest

- Belonging

- Equity.

Enthusiasm for learning can be gained by application of the DREAM model. This mnemonic stands for:

- Desire

- Relevancy

- Expectation

- Anticipation

- Motivation.

Chapter 8 Mind Map

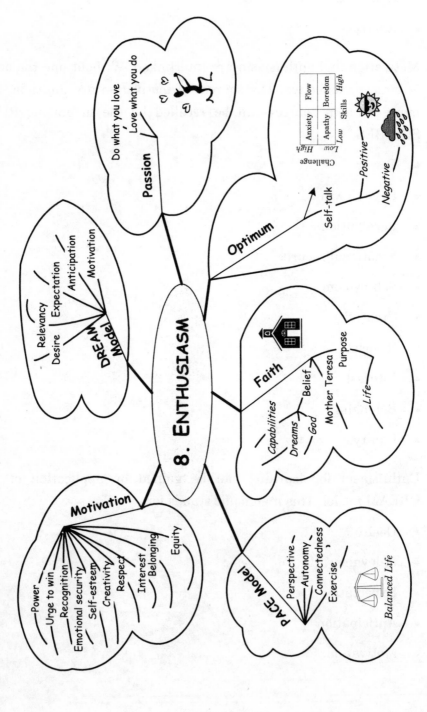

9. Discipline

> "What we do upon some great occasion will probably
> depend on what we already are. What we are will be
> the result of previous years of self-discipline."
> — Henry Parry Liddon

♦ *What is self-discipline?*

♦ *What core skills do you need to acquire for business success?*

♦ *What is the CHARISMA model of excellent companies?*

♦ *Why do companies go bust?*

♦ *What is the SUPPORT model for personal growth?*

♦ *What is the MISFILING model?*

♦ *Why do we need to discipline our emotions?*

♦ *Why is financial discipline so important?*

Self-discipline

To be successful in business we must cultivate a capacity for self-discipline. Self-discipline is the ability to pursue our desired outcomes with concentrated and focused effort. It is the discipline to forego immediate gratification for the achievement of a desired outcome in the future. It is the ability to be proactive, to think, plan and foresee potential consequences of our actions. You reap what you sow. In order to pass exams to gain recognised qualifications to help progress in your career, you need the discipline to concentrate and study. Disciplined hard work, focused on your desired outcomes will achieve your purpose.

Eleanor Roosevelt, one of the most outstanding and popular personalities of her time, said:

> In spite of a lack of special talents, one can find a way to live widely and fully. . . . I have had only three assets: I was keenly interested, I accepted every challenge and every opportunity to learn more, and I had great energy and self-discipline.

Including work there are three essentials to a successful life:

- Something to do

- Someone to love, and

- Something to look forward to.

You need purposeful activity to keep your mind occupied. Hopefully you will find this in your work. You need friendship and a special love in your life and you need to hope for the future. It is this hope that tomorrow will bring something better that keeps us going.

Internal Locus of Control

Part of self-discipline is control. Successful people have an internal locus of control. The locus of control is where we perceive the control centre of our lives to be located. People with an internal locus of control feel they are in charge of their lives. They are responsible. They adopt a can-do attitude: "If it's going to be it's up to me".

Somebody once said that there were three types of people in the world: those who make things happen, those who watch things happen and those who haven't a clue what's happening. Your aim should be to make things happen. If you don't control your own life, other people will control it for you and with their interests at heart rather than your own.

Take responsibility for your life. Undertake that MBA degree now! People with an internal locus of control draw up their own personal development and career plans. They believe they can influence the direction of their lives by undertaking formal and informal learning programmes. They don't wait around for other people to do things, they do things for themselves. They take control of their own lives and destiny. An internal locus of control is central to the concept of self-empowerment through continuous learning and self-improvement.

On the other hand, people with an external locus of control feel that they are manipulated and controlled by forces outside themselves. Consequently, they accept little personal accountability. They let their careers drift along and blame lack of progress on external forces such as the government, the boss, fate, luck, astrology, circumstances and parents. If you spend your time waiting for others to help you in your career you are going to be sorely disappointed.

Wisdom

Wisdom and self-discipline go hand in hand. There can be no real success in life without wisdom. As US columnist Abigail Van Buren put it:

> Wisdom doesn't come with old age. Nothing does — except wrinkles. It's true, some wines improve with age. But only if the grapes were good in the first place.

Wisdom has nothing got to do with IQ. People with high IQ are often emotionally immature. Data is not wisdom. Information is not wisdom. Knowledge is not wisdom.

Data, or facts and figures in their basic state, must be put in a form that can be accessed and used before you can call it information. Information must be interpreted by brainpower and experience before it becomes knowledge. Knowledge must be tempered by reflection and common sense before it becomes wisdom.

Wisdom is how effectively you use the knowledge that you know. There are many highly educated failures in the world. So what is wisdom? The following key words and phrases may give you a flavour of what's involved in wisdom:

- Soundness of judgement

- Discernment

- Insight

- Being able to see the total picture

- Ability to read situations and people

- Having good intuition

- Being objective

- Having the right priorities

- Being creative and spontaneous

- Learning from experience

- Having perspective

- Having good social skills

- Common sense

- Being of good character

- Being able to manage your money and life effectively

- Having good values and a good standard of morals

- Knowing when to persevere and knowing when to quit

- Knowing when to keep your mouth shut

- Appreciating the wonders of life

- Knowing how to avoid trouble

- Choosing the right partner in life

- Choosing the right friends.

Wisdom and the Pursuit of Happiness

Carl Jung considered the following to be the basic factors for happiness:

- Good health helps to promote happiness and happiness helps to promote good health. However, one does come across people in poor health who derive solace, acceptance and even happiness from their religious beliefs.

- The ability to have good personal and intimate relationships with your friends, family and work colleagues. We are essentially social beings and thus need a sense of belonging.

- The ability to appreciate art and nature. We are continually bombarded by the media with bad news showing the evil and destructive forces at large in the world. This conditions our mind to view human nature in a negative way. We need to seek out the good news and appreciate the inherent beauty of many things in life and the inherent goodness in people.

- An adequate standard of living and a job which offers job satisfaction and a feeling of making a positive contribution to society. Some people say that happiness is the process of being engaged in a meaningful activity. We are happy when we are developing ourselves to reach our true potential. W.B. Yeats said, "Happiness is neither virtue nor pleasure nor this thing nor that, but simple growth. We are happy when we are growing".

- A system of philosophical or religious beliefs which will help you find the meaning of life, put things in perspective and deal with the ups and downs of life.

Jung would probably despair at the modern materialistic tendency to equate happiness with the constant pursuit and accumulation of wealth and possessions.

Core Skills for Business Success

Discipline on its own is not sufficient for success in business. You also need the discipline to acquire competencies in the following areas:

- **Financial literacy** such as understanding balance sheets, cash flow statements and profit and loss accounts. You need to know the distinction between profits and cash flow and how to interpret a set of accounts using some of the well-known ratios. You need to know about the more common systems of depreciation. A knowledge of the methods of capital investment appraisal such as discounted cash flow and payback are very useful.

- **Costing**. You need to know the difference between a fixed and a variable cost and about cost allocation and absorption methods. This will give you a basis for understanding how prices are built up and how costs are apportioned to your department. An understanding of marginal costing and breakeven analysis is very useful for any manager. A knowledge of opportunity costs will help you make better decisions. All senior managers are responsible for budgets so a knowledge of budgetary control and the preparation of budgets is now almost mandatory.

- **Marketing**. Know about Michael Porter's competitive forces model, the product life cycle, the growth share matrix and the marketing mix (product, price, promotion and place). Understand sales promotion and distribution systems and generally the critical role that the marketing plan plays in strategic planning.

- **Production**. Know about recent developments in this area such as total quality management, business process re-engineering, just-in-time and world class manufacturing. Understand the implications of the learning curve and economies of scale.

- **Human relations**. Some negotiation skills are always useful and of course the ability to communicate effectively is essential. From time to time you may be called upon to make presentations. Attend a presentations skills training programme to acquire the expertise and confidence that you need. You may be called upon to sit in on interview panels and so a knowledge of the recruitment and selection process will be useful. As a manager you will be expected to have some knowledge of training and development, particularly in the areas of mentoring and coaching.

- **General business knowledge**. General legal and economic knowledge is always useful to the ambitious manager. For example, a knowledge of company law, employment legislation and the impact that variations in interest rates and foreign exchange rates have on a business are vital. Problem solving, creativity, analytical and decision-making skills are needed to be an effective manager. Learning how to acquire skills which provide the foundation for lifelong learning is essential for success in personal and business life.

- **Computer competence**. These days, ability in word processing, databases, spreadsheets and presentation graphics is a must for any manager. Keyboarding skills will give you a head start.

- **Industry knowledge**. You should have a good knowledge of the industry in which your company operates and the particular concerns such as competition and technological developments in that industry.

The SUPPORT Model

Stephen Covey's book *The Seven Habits of Highly Effective People* conceives habits as principles or strategies for effective living. My SUPPORT model is based on his ideas:

- **S**ynergise — Principle of Creative Co-operation. Synergy means that the whole is greater than the sum of its parts. Discussion and co-operation with others creates new ideas and gives new perspectives. Reread chapter 5 on Rapport. Learning sets, project work and networking should be an important part of your personal development plan.

- **U**nderstand. Seek first to understand, then to be understood — Principle of Empathic Communication. Take the other person's point of view. How would it feel if you were operating from another's perspective? Practise seeing things from a detached and another person's point of view. The meaning of communication is the response you get.

- **P**rioritise. Put first things first — Principles of Personal Management. Prioritise your actions. Operate with your prioritised purpose continually in mind. Apply the Pareto Principle to your work life. Learn and apply the principles of time management. Don't wait for things to happen, make things happen.

- **P**roactive — Principles of Personal Vision. Think ahead, take responsibility for your own life. Operate to a mission, vision, goals and plan. However, nothing is achieved without implementation.

- **O**bjectives. Begin with the end in mind — Principles of Personal Leadership. Focus your concentration on your goals and sub-goals. Break down your goals to make them more actionable and manageable.

- **R**enewal. Sharpen the saw — Principle of Balanced Self-Renewal. All work and no play makes Jack a dull boy. Some people claim it makes him a rich boy as well. But seriously, take time out for leisure pursuits and relaxation. Renew your physical, mental, social and spiritual capacities. Relax your brain by practising meditation. Live a life of balance.

- **T**hink win-win — Principle of Interpersonal Leadership. Make sure there is something there for all. Adopt an abundance mentality. Adopt an attitude of give-and-take and compromise.

These habits are interrelated. Model yourself on successful people. Practise the habits of highly effective people for greater success in your life.

The CHARISMA Model

The discipline of excellence in all aspects of business is needed for success. Peters and Waterman highlighted the key elements of successful organisations in their book *In Search of Excellence*. My model CHARISMA is based on their findings:

- **C**lose to the customer. Excellent companies are customer-orientated. They identify and respond to customer needs. In the last few years, for example, banks, insurance companies and building societies have become more customer-focused and more marketing-orientated. They are beginning to realise that it is the customer who keeps them in business.

- **H**ands-on, values-driven. Excellent companies have strong values which are shared by managers and employees. A strong common vision is shared by all. The importance of culture to the success of organisations is now readily accepted. Many organisations now publish their mission and vision statements, usually in their annual reports.

- **A**ction-oriented. Excellent companies have a bias for action, making decisions and getting things done. Many companies are now project- and team-based. They are more focused on the out-come than the process. This gives them a greater chance to ex-ploit opportunities and achieve results quickly.

- **R**emain with the business you know or stick to the knitting. Ex-cellent companies stick to their core business, the one they know best and are slow to diversify. Waterford Glass has divested away from retailing, garages and stationery and concentrated on its core business of crystal glassware.

- **I**nnovation/productivity through people. Excellent companies treat their staff with respect, often referring to them as "part-ners". Hewlett Packard is one of the leaders in the field of hu-man resource management using share-partnership schemes as a method of creating partnership with employees.

- **S**imultaneous loose-tight properties. Balance between risk and control is achieved by using appropriate levels of centralisation and decentralisation. Control is exercised more through the value system than through hierarchy. Many companies have now de-centralised in the form of strategic business units which are given a large degree of autonomy to manage their own affairs.

- **M**anagement structure — simple form, lean staff. Simplified organisation structures are now in vogue. Many organisational structures are now going through the process of simplification by delayering and outsourcing. Reduction in the number of layers of management makes for less formality, simpler work-ing, better communications and faster decision making.

- **A**utonomy and entrepreneurship. Excellent companies foster leadership and innovation. Empowerment is the name of the game. In progressive companies supervisors and managers are now adopting a more facilitating role and letting work groups manage themselves.

The MISFILING Model

Now that we have considered why companies are successful, it might be a good time to consider the flipside — why companies go bust. Survival of a business depends not so much on profits but on cash flow. A business could be making profits but still find itself short of cash to pay its bills as they fall due. In fact, some "profitable" companies have been known to go bankrupt because they literally ran out of cash. This is often due to overtrading. Overtrading is the expansion of the production and sales of a business beyond the capacity of the business to financially support it. Creditors and bankers get worried about the ability of the business to pay invoices, interest and loan repayments and they foreclose. Judging by the financial section of the daily newspapers this is not a rare occurrence.

How do companies which seem to be successful one day become insolvent and bankrupt the next? How do companies given a clear certificate of financial health from their auditors yet prove to be in financial difficulties shortly afterwards? For example, in 1990, Polly Peck announced pre-tax interim profits of £110 million, up 71 per cent on the previous year. Its cash value was estimated at over £1 billion. A month later, after a raid by the Serious Fraud Office, administrators calculated the company's worth to be minus £384 million. Like individuals, companies too must live within their means. If they spend more than they earn, sooner or later they will become insolvent.

Some companies try to keep afloat with window dressing, imprudent or even false accounting. XtraVision accounts for the year to the end of January 1990 showed a profit of £4.5 million on a turnover of £17.1 million. However, the following year, after the company had adopted a more conservative depreciation policy, the 1990 results were restated as a loss of approximately £1 million. Videos were being written off to the profit and loss account over several years instead of several months. Other companies have been brought down by overvaluing their stocks and not providing adequately for bad debts or other possible write-offs.

Nick Leeson's derivative trades brought down Barings, one of the oldest and more respected banks in the UK. A lack of financial controls on the part of the bank, and a lack of personal financial discipline on the part of Leeson, was the cocktail that led to one of the greatest banking collapses this century.

The mnemonic MISFILING will help you remember the key factors resulting in the downfall of many a company.

- **M**anagement. Small businesses in particular often have poor management structures and lack professional management expertise. They fail to adapt to a changing business climate which needs teamwork to survive rather than autocratic management. In addition, they usually have inadequate management information systems. It's a bit late in the day to find out that you have incurred a huge financial loss at the year-end. It may be too late to do something about it at that stage. These days, monthly management accounts are needed to run a business effectively. These can highlight difficulties and the need for corrective action during the year. You may have to reduce your outgoings or increase your revenue inflows if you are to stay on course to meet your budget targets. You need the information to tell you where you have been, where you are now and how to get to where you want to go.

- **I**nternal focus. Too much attention paid to internal matters, such as organisational politics, and not sufficient attention paid to customers, competitors and market conditions generally. This is caused by lack of annual business plans, marketing plans, cash budgets, budgetary control and strategic plans.

- **S**hort-termism. A preoccupation with short-term results at the expense of long-term effectiveness. The British motorcycle industry was wiped out by Japanese competition because of its short-termism and the ability of the Japanese to think strategically.

- **Financial management.** Good financial management is particularly important in the area of working capital. Problems include failure to collect debts promptly and having too much stock lying around unsold. Cash is the lifeblood of the business. Without a healthy cash flow the business will be unable to pay its day to day expenses and thus go to the wall. Overgearing is where the company is burdened by huge long-term debts. This increases its financial exposure in the form of interest and loan repayments. If revenue falls and interest rates go up, profit margins are eroded and the company may be unable to meet its interest payment. The result is that debenture holders appoint a receiver to recover their debt and this brings down the company.

- **Involvement of staff.** If you don't look after your staff they won't look after your customers. You need to get your staff involved in the decision making process. Teamwork, empowerment and profit partnership schemes are just some of the steps you can take.

- **Let down by large customer.** When the going gets tough large customers may let you down. Spread your risk by selling to many customers, getting supplies from a variety of suppliers and having a portfolio of products and investments.

- **Inadequate pricing.** Many companies get into financial trouble because they do not understand their costing structure and, therefore, charge unrealistic prices which sometimes do not recover all their costs.

- **Necessary cash flow.** Failure to generate the cash flow necessary to run the business and fund replacement and expansion plans. Overtrading occurs when a company expands its production and sales beyond the capacity of the business to generate cash flow to meet its operational expenses. It's not much use making sales if the debtors are slow to pay. In the meantime, you still have to pay the ongoing expenses of the business. No business goes bankrupt through lack of profits — all businesses go bankrupt through lack of cash. The faster a business is expanding, the sooner it will run out of cash. Cash flow is what matters in a business — when is cash received and when is cash paid out? Cash generation will lead to profit. Profit will not necessarily lead to cash generation.

- Government policies on tax, environmental and safety issues may put an unbearable financial burden on your business. You must anticipate these and build them into your plans.

Emotional IQ — Mind Discipline

An important aspect of self-discipline is emotional control. We are governed by our emotions. Most decisions have a significant emotional undertone. Most successful people have a high emotional IQ. They discipline and control their emotions. Negative feelings like spite, anger, hatred, hostility, envy, and revenge are kept in check. They have a high level of emotional maturity, introspection, influencing and social skills.

On the other hand, where these negative feelings are allowed to take root and grow disaster can ensue. For example, in the US Postal Service violence has been a serious problem for many years. On 7 May 1993, a disgruntled postal employee in California killed one employee and wounded another. In Michigan on the same day, another postal employee killed one person and wounded two others before killing himself. These deaths brought the total of killings in the USPS to 34 over the previous 10 years. In 1992 there were 396 assaults on co-workers or supervisors by postal employees. Most of the violence is committed by workers who are seeking revenge for loss of a job or a reprimand from a supervisor. These workers' feel-

ings are out of control and they have not developed their emotional
IQ.

The mnemonic SCARE will help you recall the key characteristics of emotional maturity:

- **Sensory** perception or feelings. Self-awareness and self-understanding are crucial. How can we understand other people if we don't understand ourselves? People who know themselves are more in control of their lives and have a sure sense of their identity and self-worth and where they are going in life. Knowing yourself puts you in a better position to understand and empathise with others.

- **Control.** Being in control of your emotions means you can postpone gratification and stifle impulsive behaviour. People with self-control can plan for the future and diligently pursue their goals and dreams with hard work over long periods of time. They sacrifice the present for future gain. Olympic gold medalist swimmers spend years training many hours per day, six days per week before realising their dreams. They postpone gratification by sacrificing their social life over many years for a dream of Olympic fame. All great sports achievers dream the impossible dream and then make it happen.

- **Attitude.** Psychologists have defined attitude as an internal emotional orientation that explains the actions of a person. People with a positive attitude can recover quicker from the ups and downs of life. Negative thinkers find it difficult to shake off feelings of anxiety and doom and gloom. Positive thinkers see weaknesses as potential strengths and threats as opportunities. They see problems as challenges to be overcome and mistakes as learning opportunities.

- **Relationships.** Being good at interpersonal relationships is useful in any occupation but especially for those who deal a lot with

people. These days managers need to demonstrate good communication, inspirational, leadership and teambuilding skills if
they want to succeed in their careers. They must be able to
manage difficult employees and handle conflict situations.

- **Empathy.** Empathy is being tuned into other people's feelings.
  Native Americans had a saying: "Before you criticise and choose,
  walk a mile in my shoes." These skills are particularly needed in
  the caring professions such as religion, nursing, psychology and
  management.

Lessons from the Emotional IQ

This suggests that you don't need to be a genius to be successful in
life. It highlights the importance of a disciplined mind, an even
temperament and good relationship skills to a happy and successful
life. It suggests the need to be in control of your emotions rather
than being out of control. We all have our unique strengths which
we can develop.

Conventional measures of IQ which concentrate on logical and
linguistic skills give less than half the picture. In a work context intrapersonal and interpersonal skills are just as important. Many of
the professions are high on linguistic and logical skills but ignore the
emotional, intuitive and relationship aspect of life skills. Managers
need to be aware of the necessity of developing skills in these areas.

Personal Financial Discipline

These days, with the easy availability of credit cards, it is so easy to
live beyond your means. The consumer society continually tempts
us to part with our hard-earned money. We have been brainwashed
by the consumption mentality rather than the savings mentality.
This mentality has been reinforced by the easy availability of
credit.

The secret of financial discipline, and the peace of mind that comes with it, is simply to spend less than you earn. Adopt a self-employed mentality. All expenditure should be necessary, beneficial and purposeful. Financial prudence would suggest that you save about 10 per cent of your gross income. You should reinvest the interest earned on this income. Treat your savings like capital — it's there to earn income for you rather than to be dipped into at every excuse.

To reduce risk, spread your money over different types of investments — half in government securities and the other half in blue-chip securities might be wise. You may also like to invest part of your portfolio in Post Office savings certificates which are state-guaranteed, risk-free and give a reasonable return. As a general rule there is a better return on shares than on most other types of investments provided you invest for the long term. Remember: the higher the return offered on your investments, the greater the risk. There is no such thing as a free lunch. The easiest and most painless method of saving is by deduction at source. Many organisations operate payroll deduction schemes.

Money is only important when you haven't got it. You then realise how difficult it is to get it and how reluctant people are to loan it to you. The greatest benefit of money is that it provides security for the future and peace of mind in the present. Plan now:

- What you need money for

- What you need to earn to meet your needs

- How much you need to save

- What you need to put away each month into a pension fund to provide for your retirement. Payments into a pension fund are tax-efficient up to a certain amount. Check the tax laws to see what the current position is. Remember: the majority of people are barely existing above subsistence level after they retire.

Avoid this by planning for your retirement now! Relying solely on a state pension will cater for only the most meagre existence.

Keep Accounts

Draw up a simple cash budget to plan and control your money needs. This should have two columns for each month: one for the budget and one to record the actual cash received and spent. On the top part of your cash budget list down the sources of your receipts and on the bottom part list down the items for payment. For most of us our source of income is our salary but we may have income from other sources as well. List them all. On the expenditure side we will have items such as mortgage repayments or rent, upkeep and maintenance of your house, car repayments and running costs, food costs, electricity, heating, insurance, phone, postage and so on. The difference between your cash in and cash out will be your projected surplus or deficit. If you are in the lucky position of having a projected surplus then you should plan to save some at least of this. If, on the other hand, you have a projected deficit you should examine all items of your expenditure to see which items can be reduced.

Prepare a personal balance sheet. List your assets. These consist of what you own — your house, car, furniture, savings and amounts owed to you. List your liabilities. These consist of what you owe — your mortgage, loans, and amounts owing to others for goods and services supplied. Put a value on them. For assets this will be the amount you would get for them if you sold them. For your liabilities this will be the current amount outstanding on your mortgage and other loans and invoiced values for goods and services supplied. The difference between your assets and liabilities is your net worth or equity. It's obviously best if this is a positive figure. If the difference is a minus figure, this suggests that you are nearly bankrupt or bankrupt. You immediately need to take appropriate action to put your finances on a sound footing.

Your objective should be to become debt-free. Debt attracts more debt in the form of interest and commission charges. Money attracts more money in the form of interest received. If you have a mortgage and your income increases speed up the repayments by reducing the loan term. Over a 25-year period you probably pay more than twice the capital amount of the loan in the form of interest and capital repayments. Why not save yourself thousands of pounds by increasing the monthly repayments and getting ownership of your home quicker.

Consider getting rid of some or all of your credit cards. I know they are very convenient but they do contribute to the "spend, spend, spend" mentality. They also incur substantial interest charges if the credit term is exceeded. Paying by cash often makes people more aware of money and the value for money spent. Also, paying for things when you have the surplus cash to do so means that you only buy those things that you can afford and that you never get into debt. Generally, it should be your motto to save for the things that you need, rather than get loans to purchase them. Money problems and debt are one of the chief sources of stress. You can easily eliminate this source of stress from your life by the practise of financial discipline.

The Importance of Money

Money should not be pursued for its own sake. Money is a means to an end. The biblical quotation of "the love of money is the root of all evil" is often misquoted as "money is the root of all evil". There is nothing wrong with wanting money. Money determines our standard of living and our lifestyle. Our success in life is often measured in financial terms. The house we live in, the car we drive and the education we can provide for our children are all determined by the size of our income.

Money is a reflection of the service you provide. Provide a worthwhile service that your customers need and money will follow. Pursue success and not money. However, keep the money thing in perspective. Your health is your wealth. Money may help but it is not a source of happiness. More wealth and more possessions is not a recipe for happiness. Psychologists have found that people with lots of money are not much happier than those with only enough to survive. It's what you can do with money to make other people happy that will be a source of satisfaction and happiness in your life rather than the accumulation of wealth.

Generally, people's expenses rise to meet their income if they don't practise financial prudence. Many people, as they get promoted, just adjust their lifestyle upwards to the greater source of income. There is nothing wrong with this provided you do it within your means and stick to your habit of saving about 10 per cent of your income. Remember that you may not always be earning big money. In the future, poor health, redundancy, divorce and so on may all drain your financial resources. It is at times like this that you will appreciate the fact that you have put money away into savings.

When buying items like shoes, clothes, furniture and equipment buy quality. It lasts longer, and such purchases will save you money in the long term. Bargains look attractive but they are often fool's gold. They entice you to buy things that you don't really need. Don't lend money to relatives. They won't appreciate it and you'll probably have difficulty getting it back, often causing resentment in the process. After all, you are not in the lending business. That is the function of banks! If you must give them money, and you can afford to do so, make it a gift. In that way you will retain friendships and avoid unpleasantness in the future.

Look for opportunities to make money. Mix with successful people. These people will show you what it takes to make and, more importantly, how to retain money. Money should be used for investment and to generate further wealth. Some people who become millionaires on the lotto don't know what to do with their newly acquired wealth and proceed to spent it as fast as possible. They often feel guilty with such huge sums of money, and it brings them problems and grief rather than happiness. Adopt an abundance mentality and a positive mental mindset as far as money is concerned. There is always enough money to go around. It's a question of identifying needs and providing a product or service to meet those needs to generate the income desired.

Simplify Your Life

Over the years we are inclined to accumulate possessions in our life. Many of these possessions seem to be useful when we first bought them but now play no part in our life. The consumer society encourages us to spend on trivia. However, instead of doing a spring cleaning on a regular basis we tend to hoard things, thinking that they may come in useful some day. We all have a magpie instinct. That day never arrives and so our homes, attics, places underneath the stairs and garages all become cluttered up with rubbish.

Remove clutter from your life. Give away or throw out anything that you do not need. Some of the stuff may be of value to someone else and could be donated to charitable organisations or even sold off. A car boot sale might be the solution! Simplify your life and concentrate on those possessions that provide a real usefulness to your existence. The less clutter about you the easier it will be to find the things that you need when you need them. A tidy home facilitates a tidy mind.

Summary

Self-discipline is an important characteristic of successful people. Self-discipline is the ability to stick to a task and see it through to the end. However, it needs to be tempered with personal and business type skills. The core skills for business success were identified. The SUPPORT model for personal success was discussed. This stands for:

- Synergise

- Understand

- Prioritise

- Proactive

- Objectives

- Renewal

- Think win-win.

The CHARISMA model was used to highlight the characteristics of highly successful companies. This mnemonic stands for:

- Close to the customer

- Hands-on, value-driven

- Action-oriented

- Remain with the business you know

- Innovation/productivity through people

- Simultaneous loose–tight relationships

- Management structure — simple form/lean staff

- Autonomy and entrepreneurship.

The mnemonic MISFILING will help you remember the key factors leading to the downfall of many a company:

- Management

- Internal focus

- Short-termism

- Financial management

- Involvement of staff

- Let down by large customer

- Inadequate pricing

- Necessary cash flow

- Government policies.

Keeping your emotions in check is an important aspect of self-discipline. The key aspect of emotional IQ can be recalled by the mnemonic SCARE. This stands for:

- Sensory perception and feelings

- Control

- Attitude

- Relationships

- Empathy.

Financial discipline or living always within your means guarantees solvency and peace of mind. This applies to personal as well as corporate financial situations. Spend more than you earn and eventually you will be on the road to financial ruin.

Chapter 9 Mind Map

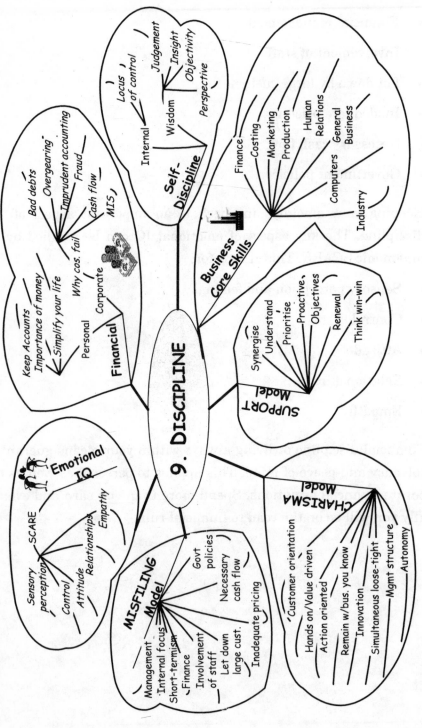
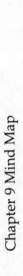

10. Putting It All Together

"What is the recipe for successful achievement? To my mind there are just four essential ingredients: Choose a career you love, give it the best there is in you, seize your opportunities, and be a member of a team."
— Benjamin F. Fairless

The DESCRIBED Model

The DESCRIBED model of personal and business excellence is a synthesis of the best available information on success drawn from psychology, neurolinguistic programming, learning principles, strategic thinking, finance, business management and ethics. If you model yourself on the effective behaviours of successful people, you too can become a success in your life. DESCRIBED is the model for success and a memory jogger which stands for:

- **De**termination

- **E**steem

- **S**trategic thinking

- **C**ommunication

- **R**apport

- **I**deals

- **B**elief

- **E**nthusiasm

- **D**iscipline.

To adopt the successful behaviours outlined in this book you need to put them into practice. Mere reading is not sufficient. You must walk the talk. Therefore this book is not the kind of book that you can read in one sitting and then get on with your life. To benefit from the book you need to revisit it on an ongoing basis for reflection and action. Actions must be practised for a considerable period of time before they become habits. Until you've arrived at the unconscious competence stage you haven't really learned. To arrive at this stage requires constant practice and reflection.

The DESCRIBED Model for Personal Excellence

Determination

If you want to succeed in personal life and your business career you need determination and purpose. Winners are those who refuse to quit. Successful people are energetic and need plenty of stamina for the long hours that are necessary to invest over many years to achieve worthwhile goals. Nothing worthwhile in life is achieved without dedicated application. To succeed in life we need to be able to cope with constant change and to frequently update our skills and knowledge. The ASPIRE model is a memory jogger for the key aspects of a self-development plan:

- **A**ssess your current position
- **S**WOT analysis
- **P**lan
- **I**mplement
- **R**eview
- **E**valuate.

To cope with constant change we need to be able to frequently update skills and knowledge. This requires a dedication to lifelong learning. To equip you for this task, an awareness of the latest thinking in learning, such as the types of learning, the learning stages model, the learning cycle and the styles of learning, will prove to be very useful in your search for personal excellence.

Esteem

Our self-esteem determines how successful and happy we are in our lives. Self-esteem is one of the key characteristics of successful people. Being assertive and knowing your rights will enhance your self-esteem. An understanding of multiple intelligence will increase your sense of self-worth. To enhance your self-esteem you must focus on change from within before you change your behaviour style when dealing with others. Visualisations, affirmations and modelling the self-esteem of highly effective people are some of the strategies you could adopt to improve your self-esteem.

The multiple intelligence theory should be a great source of joy and inspiration to all of us. This theory suggests that each of us has a wide range of potential abilities awaiting development which is a great reason for valuing ourselves more and increasing our sense of self-worth. We really should go about exploiting these great gifts. The SIMILAR mnemonic is a memory jogger for recalling these marvellous abilities:

- **S**patial
- **I**nterpersonal
- **M**usical
- **I**ntrapersonal
- **L**inguistic
- **A**nalytical
- **R**eflex.

Strategic Thinking

To progress to senior management positions in business you need to be able to think strategically. The helicopter viewpoint is the ability to see the big picture. The eight Ps of success in business management are:

- **P**urpose
- **P**lan
- **P**assion
- **P**rinciple
- **P**roduct
- **P**osition
- **P**rofit
- **P**eople.

Knowing the SPEWSIC model is one of the key ways to help you think strategically. SPEWSIC is a memory jogger for the key steps in strategic planning:

- **S**trategic objectives

- **P**osition audit

- **E**nvironmental analysis

- **W**ots up analysis

- **S**trategies to fill the gap

- **I**mplementation

- **C**ontrol.

Common business strategies include organic growth, growth by acquisition, mergers, buyout and strategic alliances. An understanding of strategic business models such, as the PLC and the BCG, will enhance your ability to think in strategic terms.

Communication

Managers spend most of their day communicating. The PICTURE and GRAPEVINE models are wonderful memory joggers for the key aspects of communication.

PICTURE stands for:

- **P**itch

- **I**nflexion

- **C**ourtesy

- **T**one

- **U**nderstanding

- **R**ate

- **E**nunciation.

GRAPEVINE stands for:

- **G**esture

- **R**ecurring pauses

- **A**ppearance

- **P**osture

- **E**ye contact

- **V**oice

- **I**nvolve the listener

- **N**atural self

- **E**ntertaining.

An understanding of how perceptions are formed will help us to become better communicators. Most of us are not aware of how faulty and limiting our perceptions can be and how they can influence our behaviour. Knowing about the halo effect, stereotyping and cognitive dissonance should help you become a better communicator. Language can limit your communication and achievement in life. Find out your own thinking and language preferences and notice how others express their thoughts. Language can be used to enhance or distort a message. Good communication skills are needed by managers in negotiations, meetings, interviews, coaching, counselling and mentoring.

Rapport

Rapport is a feeling of harmony with yourself and others. Being able to see things from other people's viewpoint and to empathise with them is a critical business skill. Remembering people's names is a quick and easy way to win the rapport of others provided that you adopt a simple process known as the MEMORY jogger which stands for:

- **M**inutes not seconds

- **E**valuate

- **M**ake an effort

- **O**rganise

- **R**epeat

- **Y**our curiosity.

If you apply the techniques for matching words, voice and body language you will improve your ability to create rapport with other people. You must achieve harmony with yourself before you can proceed to create harmony with others. Reframing is a technique for evaluating past experiences and reinterpreting them in a more favourable light. Your imagination is the greatest resource you have.

The Johari Window is a model which will improve your ability to be more open with yourself and with others. A knowledge of the different behaviour styles of people will help you improve your ability to build rapport with others.

Ideals

Ideals are about ethics. Ethics is an attempt to determine moral standards or rules that ought to govern human conduct, the values worth adopting, and the character traits worth developing in personal and business life. Therefore, ethics attempts to see what rules, codes, values, and standards ought to be adopted for morally right behaviour, integrity and truthfulness in human situations. Ethical systems, even in different cultures, virtually all accept that any action injurious to another is wrong.

Many a political and business career has been ruined by an abuse of ethics. Presidents have fallen and chief executives jailed because of an abuse of ethics. The importance of the application of good ethical standards in a business cannot be overstressed. Ethics are monitored by the law, professions, the media and environmental groups. Many professions have drawn up their own codes of ethics. Most large organisations have drawn up their own code of ethics to guide the conduct of management and employees in business dealings.

Belief

People move in the direction of their dominant thoughts. Our beliefs, values and attitudes determine what we become. You can programme your mind with positive beliefs. The SAVER model is a mental jogger for recalling the steps in programming your mind for success:

- **S**ubstitute positive for negative thoughts

- **A**ffirm

- **V**isualise

- **E**motionalise

- **R**ehearse.

Fears often keep us back from achieving our goals. Fear of failure, fear of change and fear what other people will think of us are some of the common fears confronting us. Most of our fears are never realised. Fear has been defined as **F**alse **E**vidence **A**ppearing **R**eal.

The environment, behaviour, capability, beliefs, identity and spirituality are all interlinked and determine the effectiveness and success of your life.

The core beliefs for business success are:

- The philosophy of customer-orientation

- Total quality management

- Zero defects and getting it right first time

- Continuous improvement

- Lifelong learning

- The learning organisation

- Empowerment

- People are your most important asset.

Enthusiasm

Do what you love and love what you do. Enthusiasm is a passion for what you do. Without enthusiasm there is little chance of true success in personal and professional life. Work activities which offer a high challenge and use a high level of skills create flow or optimum work satisfaction. Enthusiasm must be supported by faith and motivation.

Faith is a belief in your capabilities, your dreams and the providence of God. Faith is belief without evidence — belief that you can achieve a goal without knowing exactly how you're going to do it. All the great achievements and inventions in history would have been impossible without faith.

Enthusiastic people are mostly motivated by moving towards the achievement of positive and attractive goals rather than the need to avoid pain or punishment. They like challenge and responsibility and take pride in their work.

Just like any other area of life to be successful in learning you need plenty of enthusiasm. The DREAM model is a good memory jogger for the key characteristics of building enthusiasm for learning:

- **D**esire

- **R**elevancy

- **E**xpectation
- **A**nticipation
- **M**otivation.

Discipline

The discipline of hard work and the ability to cope with disappointments are the core characteristics of successful people. Self-discipline is the ability to stick to a task and see it through to the end. In addition to self-discipline, to be truly successful you need wisdom. Wisdom is discernment, learning from experience and emotional maturity. However, discipline and wisdom need to be tempered with personal and business skills. The SUPPORT model for personal success is:

- **S**ynergise
- **U**nderstand
- **P**rioritise
- **P**roactive
- **O**bjectives
- **R**enewal
- **T**hink win-win.

The CHARISMA model for business success is:

- **C**lose to the customer
- **H**ands-on, value-driven
- **R**emain with the business you know
- **I**nnovation/productivity through people
- **S**imultaneous loose–tight relationships

- **M**anagement structure — simple form/lean staff.

- **A**utonomy and entrepreneurship.

The mnemonic MISFILING is a memory jogger for helping you re-member the key factors leading to the downfall of many a company:

- **M**anagement

- **I**nternal focus

- **S**hort-termism

- **F**inancial management

- **I**nvolvement of staff

- **L**et down by large customer

- **I**nadequate pricing

- **N**ecessary cash flow

- **G**overnment policies.

Keeping your emotions in check is an important aspect of self-discipline. The key aspect of emotional IQ can be recalled by the mnemonic SCARE. This stands for:

- **S**ensory perception and feelings

- **C**ontrol

- **A**ttitude

- **R**elationships

- **E**mpathy.

Financial discipline or living always within your means guarantees solvency and peace of mind. This applies to personal as well as cor-porate financial situations. Spend more than you earn and eventu-ally you will be on the road to financial ruin.

I'd like to end with a quote from Ralph Waldo Emerson who says that the real test of success is:

> To laugh often and much; to win the respect of intelligent people and the affection of children; to earn the appreciation of honest critics and endure the betrayal of false friends; to appreciate beauty, to find the best in others; to leave the world a bit better, whether by a healthy child, a garden patch or a redeemed social condition; to know even one life has breathed easier because you have lived. This is to have succeeded.

God bless you and good luck in your quest for success!

Chapter 10 Mind Map

10 DESCRIBED

9. Discipline
- Personal
- Corporate
- Financial

1. Determination
- Persistence
- Stamina
- Change
- Learning Styles

2. Esteem
- PMA
- Affirmations
- Visualisations
- Assertiveness
- Multiple IQ

3. Strategic Thinking
- 8 Ps
- SPEWSIC
- Start
- Finish

4. Communication
- Perception
- Conflict
- Language

5. Rapport
- Personal
- With others
- Trust
- Johari Window

6. Ideals
- Ethics
- Codes
- Training
- Stakeholders

7. Belief
- Empowering
- SFP
- Disempowering
- Placebo Effect
- Mind-Body

8. Enthusiasm
- Motivation
- Positive Self-Talk
- Faith
- Passion

Bibliography

Alder, Harry (1996) NLP for Trainers: Communicating for Excellence. London: McGraw Hill.

Andreas, Steve and Faulkner, Charles (1996) *NLP: The New Technology of Achievement*, London: Nicholas Brealey.

Armstrong, Michael (1993) *A Handbook of Personnel Management Practice*, London: Kogan Page

Belbin, Meredith (1996) *Team Roles at Work*, Oxford: Butterworth-Heinemann

Bishop, Sue (1996) *Develop Your Assertiveness*, London: Kogan Page.

Blake, Robert R. and Mouton, Jane S. (1964) *The Managerial Grid*, Houston: Gulf.

Bland, Glenn (1996) *The Power of Thought: Ageless Secrets of Great Achievement*, Rocklin, MD: Prima.

Blakeslee, Thomas R. (1997) *The Attitude Factor: Extend Your Life by Changing the Way You Think*, London: Thorsons.

Braham, Barbara J. (1995) *Creating a Learning Organisation*, London: Kogan Page.

Branden, Nathen (1994) *The Six Pillars of Self-Esteem*, New York: Bantam.

Carlson, Richard (1998) *Don't Worry, Make Money: Spiritual and Practical Ways to Create Abundance and More Fun in Your Life*, London: Hodder and Stoughton.

Chapman, Elwood N. (1987) *How to Develop a Positive Attitude*, London: Kogan Page.

Christopher, Elizabeth M. (1996) *Negotiating Skills for Business*, London: Kogan Page.

Clements, Phil. (1995) *Be Positive*, London: Kogan Page.

Cole, G A. (1994) *Strategic Management*, London: DP Publications.

Covey, Stephen R. (1989) *The Seven Habits of Highly Effective People*, London: Simon & Schuster.

Csikszentmihalyi, Mihaly (1991) *Flow: The Psychology of Optimal Experience*, New York: HarperCollins.

Cullinan, Kay. (1996) *Practical Communication*, Dublin: Irish Management Institute.

Dean, Amy E. (1997) *Growing Older, Growing Better: Daily Meditations for Celebrating Aging*, Carlsbad, CA: Hay House.

Decker, Bert (1988) *How to Communicate Effectively*, London: Kogan Page.

Denny, Richard (1997) *Succeed for Yourself. Unlock your Potential for Success and Happiness*, London: Kogan Page.

Detmartini, Dr. John F. (1997) *Count Your Blessings: The Healing Power of Gratitude and Love*, Rockport, IL: Element Books.

Fenchuk, Gary W. (1995) *Timeless Wisdom: Thoughts on life ...the way it should be*, Richmond, VA: Cake Eaters, Inc.

Ferguson, Jan (1996) *Perfect Assertiveness*, London: Arrow Books Ltd.

Fletcher, John (1995) *Conducting Effective Interviews*, London: Kogan Page.

Gardiner, Howard (1993) *Frames of Mind: The Theory of Multiple Intelligences*. London: Fontana.

Goleman, Daniel (1995) *Emotional Intelligence*, London: Bloomsbury.

Grossman, Ned (1994) *How to Succeed in Life: Ideas and Principles They Don't Teach in School*, Columbus, OH: Diamond.

Gutmann, Joanna (1993) *The Assertiveness Workbook: A plan for busy women*, London: Sheldon.

Harrison, Rosemary (1992) *Employee Development*, London: Institute of Personnel Management.

Haynes, Marion E. (1988) *Effective Meeting Skills*, London: Kogan Page.

Hoffman, Michael and Moore, Jennifer Mills (1990) *Business Ethics: Readings And Cases in Corporate Morality*, New York, McGraw Hill.

Holden, Philip (1996) *Super Success: Discover Your True Potential and Get What You Want out of Life*, London: Piatkus.

Honey, Peter (1994) *101 Ways to Develop Your People, Without Really Trying: A Manager's Guide to Work-based Learning*, Berkshire. Published by Dr. Peter Honey.

IBE (The Institute of Business Ethics) (1992) *Business Ethics and Company Codes. Current Best Practice in the UK*, London: Institute of Business Ethics.

Johnson, Rex and Swindley, David (1995) *Awaken Your Inner Power: How to Discover the Secrets of Health, Happiness & Success*, Shaftesbury: Element Books.

Keyes, Ken, Jr. (1997) *Handbook to Higher Consciousness*, Middlesex: Eden Grove.

Lewis, Philip V. (1985) "Defining 'Business Ethics': Like Nailing Jello to a Wall", *Journal of Business Ethics*, Volume 4, Pages 377-383.

Lindenfield, Gael (1992) *Assert Yourself*, London: Thorsons.

Maddux, Robert B. (1988) *Successful Negotiation*, London: Kogan Page.

Malone, Samuel A. (1997) *Mind Skills for Managers*, Aldershot: Gower.

Malone, Samuel A. (1997) *How to Set Up and Manage a Corporate Learning Centre*, Aldershot: Gower.

Malone, Samuel A. (1996) *Learning to Learn*, London: CIMA

Malone, Samuel A. (1993) "Ethical Issues in HRM", Unpublished Assignment for M.Ed Degree of University of Sheffield.

McGinnis, Alan Loy (1997) *The Balanced Life: Achieving Success in Work and Love*, Minneapolis, MN: Augsburg Fortress.

Molden, David (1996) *Managing with the Power of NLP: Neuro-linguistic Programming for Competitive Advantage*, London: Pitman.

Morris, Tom (1994) *True Success: How to Achieve Excellence & Fulfilment in all Areas of Your Life*, London: Piatkus.

Mumford, Alan (1997) (Third Edition) *Management Development Strategies for Action*, London: Institute of Personnel and Development.

O'Connor, Joseph and Seymour, John (1994) *Training with NLP: Skills for Managers, Trainers and Communicators*, London: Thorsons.

Palladino, Connie D. (1989) *Developing Self-Esteem*, London: Kogan Page.

Pedler, Mike, Burgoyne, John, Boydell, Tom (1994) *A Manager's Guide to Self-Development*, London: McGraw-Hill.

Peters, Tom and Waterman, Robert (1982) *In Search of Excellence*, New York and London: Harper & Row

Quben, Nido R. (1997) *Stairway to Success: The Complete Blueprint for Personal and Professional Achievement*, New York: Wiley.

Quilliam, John (1996) *Psychology and Work*, Dublin: Irish Management Institute.

Samways, Louise (1997) *The 12 Secrets of Health and Happiness*, Melbourne: Penguin Books Australia Ltd.

Smither, Robert D, Houston, John M and McIntire, Sandra D. (1996) *Organisation Development Strategies for Changing Environments*, New York: HarperCollins College.

Sommer, Bobbe (1993) *Psycho-Cybernetics 2000*, Elizabeth, NJ: Prentice Hall.

Spooner, Peter (1992) "The Changing Face of Corporate Responsibility", *Annual Review of International Management Practice*, Brussels: Management Centre Europe.

Stubbes, David R. (1985) *Assertiveness at Work: A Necessary Guide to an Essential Skill*, London: Pan Books.

Turner, Colin (1994) *Born to Succeed: How to Release Your Unlimited Potential*, Shaftesbury: Element.

Turner, Colin (1997) *Swimming with Piranhas Makes You Hungry: How to Simplify Your Life and Achieve Financial Independence*, Bristol: InToto Books.

Waters, Michael (1996) *Dictionary of Personal Development*, Shaftesbury, Element.

Williams, Dr. Sid E. (1996) *Lasting Purpose: A Mindset for Success*, Deerfield Beach, FL: Health Communications.

Index

3M Corporation, 75

abundance mentality, 37, 191, 239
acceptance, 7
accommodating conflict style, 94
accountancy bodies, 175
accounting
    practice, standard statements of
        (SSAPs), 176
accounts, keeping personal, 236-7
acid rain, 161, 170
acquisition strategies, 62-3
acting good/bad guy negotiation
    strategy, 104
action
    -oriented culture, 227-8
    learning, 47
    plans, 26, 39
    points and meetings, 108
activist learning, 16-9
    improving, 20-1
ACTRESS mnemonic, the, 72-3
adjustment in selection, 121
advertising issues, 160, 179
adversity, overcoming, 4-5
advocate mentoring role, 111-2
affirmations, 193-6, 209
    learning, 194
    interpersonal relations, 195-6
    personal success, 194-5
ageism, 160
agenda,
    closed, 114
    hidden, 21
    open, 114
affirmations, 39

aggressive behaviour, 42-3, 94
aha! experience, 29
Alaskan oil spill, 167-9
Ali, Muhammad, 47
alcohol, 33
Alzheimer's disease, 193
analytical intelligence, 47
anchoring, 39
angel's advocate, 112
anger, 6, 94
animal welfare, 171-2
Animal Liberation Movement (ALM),
    171
anticipation of learning, 216
annual business plans, 54
apartheid, 160
apparent withdrawal negotiation
    strategy, 103-4
appearance in communication, 84
appraisal interview, 123-7
    after the, 125
    before the, 124
    during the, 124-5
appraisal, performance, 113, 123-7
appraiser coaching role, 119
aptitudes in selection, 121
arbitration, 93
Aristotle, 46, 145
asbestos, 161, 169
as-if model, 40
ASPIRE mnemonic of a self-
    development plan, the, 10-2, 245
assertiveness, 24
    and self-esteem, 42-5
attitudes, 91, 99, 209, 233
    negative, 9, 12, 127, 191

attitudes (cont'd)
  positive, 37, 189
attribution theory, 86-7
audit committees, 177
auditory state, 140
autonomous
  maintenance, 201
  work groups, 201
autonomy, 212-3, 228
avoiding conflict style, 95
away people, 150

Bach, R., 185
Bader, D.,4
bait and switch, 179
balance sheets, 67, 224
Bannister, R., 189
Baring's Bank, 230
Bay of Pigs, 89
BCCI, 167
Beatles, the, 46
von Beethoven, L., 46
Belbin, M., 109
Belfast Agreement, 104
belief, 185-206
beliefs, 91, 97-9, 203-4
  for better business performance,
    197-201, 250-1
  and learning, integrated nature of,
    201-3
beliefs, 10, 250-1
  disempowering, 187-8
  empowering, 188-9
behaviour, 202-3
  and the SAVER mnemonic, 203
belonging and motivation, 214
Bennis, W., 137
Best, G., 47
Bhopal disaster, 167-9
biodegradable packaging, 170, 179
Blake and Mouton's Managerial Grid,
  23
body
  language, 21, 83, 101, 121, 123, 128
  movements, 141-2
Body Shop, 170
Boston Consulting Group (BCG), 68

matrix, 68-9
Bovril, 67
brainstorming, 19, 198
brainwashing, 179
Branson, R., 2, 55
break-even analysis, 23
breathing in communication, 142
bribery, 156, 161, 166
Brief History of Time, A, 4
British Institute of Management
  (BIM), 162
budgets, 47, 54, 236
business
  knowledge, general, 225
  plans, annual, 54
  performance, beliefs for better,
    197-201, 250-1
  process re-engineering, 29, 91, 224
  strategies, 65-6
  success, core skills for, 224-5
Butler, E.B., 207
buyouts, management, 66

Cadbury report on corporate
  governance, 177
capability, 203
capital
  equipment audit, 58
  investment appraisal, 224
car industry, 169
Carroll, L., 51
case studies, 16
cash
  cow products, 68
  flow, 55, 65, 68, 224, 231-2
    discounted (DCF), 23, 71
  traps, 69
CATS mnemonic on mentoring roles,
  the, 111-2
cause and effect
  in communication, 97-8
  diagrams, 23
cause and effect , the law of, 158
cellular manufacturing processes, 201
Centre for Policy research, 164
chairman, role of, 106-7, 110
challenge, 209

change, planning, 8-10
Chaplin. C., 47
character, the importance of, 157-9
CHARISMA mnemonic of excellent
companies, the, 227-8, 252-3
Chernobyl, 167
chlorofluorocarbons (CFCs), 161,
    169-70
CHOICE mnemonic, the, 74-6
churning, 167
Churchill, W., 47
cigarette industry, 167-8
Clinton, Pres. W.J., 24, 47, 83
coaching, 116-9, 225
co-counselling, 84
cognitive dissonance, 88
collaborating conflict style, 95
comfort zone, the, 14-5
comfort zones, 13-5, 25
commitment, 3, 9, 27
communicating in negotiation, 101-2
communication, 81-135, 247-8
    empathic, principle of, 226
    the GRAPEVINE mnemonic of,
        83-5
    importance of, 81-2
    the PICTURE mnemonic of, 82-3
communicator
    coaching role, 118
    mentoring role, 111
Companies Acts, 175-6
company worker role, 110
competence,
    conscious, 26
    unconscious, 26-7, 203
competing conflict style, 94
competition,
    unfair, 161
competitive forces model, 224
compromising conflict style, 95
computer competence, 11, 15, 24, 48,
    203, 225
concentric diversification, 63
conciliation, 93
conflict
    grid, the, 94
    of interest, 160

styles, 93-5
conflict,
    interpersonal, 90-1
    organisational, 91-2
    resolving, 92-3
conglomerate diversification, 63
connectedness, 213
conscious
    competence, 26
    incompetence, 26-7, 203
constructive self-talk, 193-6
Consultative Committee of
    Accountancy Bodies (CCAB), 176
consumer products, safe, 161
consumerism, 169
continuous improvement, 19, 22, 27-8,
    38, 196, 198
control
    and risk, balance between, 228
    of strategies, 72-3
control,
    emotional, 233
    internal locus of, 220-1
controls, 197-8
Coolidge, Pres. C., 2
co-operation, principle of creative, 226
core
    beliefs for business success,
        197-201, 250-1
    business, concentration on, 228
    manager's potential, 126-7
corporate
    social reporting, 177
    venturing, 66
corruption, 160-1, 166
Cortisol, 193
cost-benefit analysis, 23
costing knowledge, 224
counselling interview, 121-3
    after the, 123
    before the, 122
    during the, 122-3
courtesy in communication, 82
Covey, S.R., 155, 226
creativity, 18, 52, 73, 198
    and motivation, 214
crisis management, 19

critical path analysis, 23, 74
Csikszentmihalyi, M., 209
Cuba, 89
culture, company, 91, 115, 227-8
customer
    orientation, 55, 197, 227
    service, 55-6
customers,
    internal and external, 197
    large, desertion of, 231

da Vinci, L., 45
Dalkon shield, 167
deadlines negotiation strategy, 104
deadwood potential, 127
debt, 56-7, 60, 237
de Gaulle, C.,
decision trees, 23
deletions in communication, selective,
    96
demographic environment, 59
demonstrations, 16
denial, 6
depression, 7, 41
DESCRIBED model for personal
    excellence, the, xiii-v, 243-4
desire for learning, 215
determination, 1-32, 244-5
devil's advocate, 88, 111
Diana, Princess, 46
different strokes for different folks,
    150-2
differentiation, product, 64
diffusion
    analysis, 70-1
    of innovation curve, 70-1
disabled, the, 160
disappointment, 6
disciplinary interview, 129-31
    after the, 131
    before the, 130
    during the, 130-1
discipline, 93, 219-42, 252-3
    personal financial, 234-6
discounted cash flow (DCF), 23, 71
discrimination, 160
disempowering beliefs, 187-8

Disney, W., 2, 142
dissonance, cognitive, 88
distortions in communication, 97
diversification, 62-3
    concentric, 63
    conglomerate, 63
    horizontal, 62
    vertical, 62-3
divestment, 66, 68, 228
dog products, 68
dream, 10
    the impossible dream, 189-90
DREAM mnemonic for enthusiasm to
    learn, the, 215-6, 251-2
driving forces, 7-8
drug abuse, 33

Earthwatch, 170
ecological environment, 59
economic
    environment, 59
    rights for women, 160
Edison, T.A., 11, 37, 47
eight Ps of success, 54-6
Einstein, A., 142, 193
electromagnetic fields, 161, 170-1
Emerson, R.W., 185, 254,
emotional
    IQ, 232-4
        lessons from the, 234
    security and motivation, 214
emotionalisation of success, 196
empathy, 38, 118, 142, 234
empowering beliefs, 188-9
empowerment, 55, 93, 200-1, 215, 228,
    231
endorphins, 193
entertaining in communication, 84-5
enthusiasm, 9, 45, 207-18, 251-2
    for learning, 215-6
        DREAM mnemonic for, 215-6
entrepreuneurship, 52, 228
enunciation in communication, 83
environmental
    accounting and auditing, 177
    analysis, 58-9
    groups, 170-1

issues, 161, 231
  protection, 160-1
  stress, 91
Environmental Protection Agency, 168
environmentalism, 169
equality, 160
equipment audit, 58
equity and motivation, 214
esteem, 33-50, 245-6
ethical
  environment, 59
  standards, legally required, 175-6
  statements, 55
ethics
  audit, 173-4
  in general management, 178-9
  in human resource management,
    177-8
  implemented?, how is, 172-3
  in marketing, 179
  and power, 162-3
  relevant?, where is, 177-82
  and stakeholders, 179-81
  training, 173-4
ethics, 156-7
  business, 181-2
  business?, why, 164
  codes of, 161-2, 173-4
  positive, 169-70
  surveys of, 164-6
  unethical, 55, 165
  what is, ?, 159-60
  why, ?, 163-4
European Social Charter, 175
evaluation, 12
evaluator role, 110
Excellence, In Search of, 227
exercise, 213
expectation of learning, 216
experience in selection, 120
experiential learning, 16-7
experimentation learning, 17-8
exploring negotiating options, 102-3
Exxon, 168-9
eye
  contact in communication, 84
  movements, 141

factual question, 99
fait accompli negotiation strategy, 103
faith, 210-1
fear, 35, 186-7
feedback, 117
financial
  audit, 57
  discipline, personal, 234-6
  literacy, 225
  management, 231
  reporting standards (FRSs), 176
finisher role, 110
fish kills, 161, 171
FISTIC mnemonic for a good speech,
  the, 106
Flatley, M., 47
Fleming, Sir A., 3
FLOOR mnemonic of question types,
  the, 99-100

flow charts, 23, 45, 48
Ford, H., 12, 17, 55, 144
force-field analysis, 7-8, 23
forming, group, 108
four P agenda, 107-8
four-stage model of learning, 24-7
Frames of Mind, 45
Francis, C., 208
franchising, 65
Franklin, B., 102
Freud, S., 46
Friends of the Earth, 170
Fry, A., 75
Fulton, R., 76

Galileo, 29
Gandhi, M., 142
Gardiner, H., 45
general
  business knowledge, 225
  management and ethics, 178-9
generalisations in communication, 98
genetically-modified (GM) foods, 161,
  180
gesture in communication, 83
goals, 3, 10-2, 39, 53-4, 103, 123-5
Gone with the Wind, 2

government policies, 232
GRAPEVINE mnemonic for communicating, the, 83-5, 248
gratification, immediate, 35
Green movement, the, 170
Greenpeace, 170
grievance
    interview, 127-9
    procedures, 93
group
    development and the Johari Window, 150
    dynamics and meetings, 108-9
    invulnerability, 89
    moral blindness, 89
    norms, 91
    nullification of divergent views, 89
    oppression, 89
    rationalisation, 89
    roles at meetings, 109-10
    solidarity, 89
    stereotyping, 89
    think, 88-9
growth share matrix, 23, 68-9, 224
Guinness Light, 67

habits, 157, 202
halo effect, 85, 120
hamburger technique in appraisal, 125
hands-on culture, 227
Handy, C., 88, 147
happiness, 193
    wisdom and the pursuit of, 223-4
harassment, sexual, 160
Harvard Business School, 178
Hawaii, 89
Hawking, S., 4
health and safety issues, 160
helicopter viewpoint, 53-4
Heraclitus, 6, 157
Herald of Free Enterprise, The, 169
Hewlett Packard, 228
Hierarchy of Needs, Maslow's,
Hoffman, M., 164
Honda, 169
honesty, 155-7

Honey, P., 18, 20
horizontal diversification, 62
horn effect, 85, 120
human relations skills, 225
human resource management and ethics, 177-8
human resources audit, 57
Hume, J., 3
humour, 37, 84

iceberg model, 92
ideal team worker role, 110
ideals, 155-183, 249-50
identity, 204
imagination, 5, 9
immediate gratification, 35
implementation, 11
    of strategies, 71-2
improvement, continuous, 19, 22, 27-8, 38, 198
incentive programmes, 198
incompetence,
    conscious, 25-6
    unconscious, 25
incremental learning, 28
Industrial Society, the, 107
industry knowledge, 225
inflexion in communication, 82
information deficiency, 90-1
Ingram, H., 147
initiative, 52, 73
inner
    dialogue, 144
    peace, 143
innovation through people, 228
inside-reference people, 151
insider dealing, 160
Institute of Business Ethics, 173-5
Institute of Chartered Accountants in Ireland, 176
intelligence quotient (IQ), 49, 221
    emotional, 232-4
intelligences, multiple, 45-9, 188
interest and motivation, 214
internal audit, 176
interpersonal
    conflict, 90-1

intelligence, 46, 48
leadership, principle of, 227
relationship skills, 24, 91, 93, 102,
    121, 233
internal
    audit, 176
    checks
    controls
    focus, 230
interview,
    appraisal, 123-7
    counselling, 121-3
    disciplinary, 129-31
    grievance, 127-9
    selection, 119-21, 225
intrapersonal intelligence, 46, 48
intuition, 144
investigator of resources role, 110
involving
    the listener, 84
    staff, 231
invulnerability, group, 89

Jackins, H., 84
James, W., 12
Janis, I., 89
Japan, 166
Japanese strategic thinking, 230-1
job
    dissatisfaction, 209
    enlargement, 200, 214
    enrichment, 200, 214
    restructuring, 93
    rotation, 48, 200-1, 214
    satisfaction, 208, 223
Johari Window, 147-50
    and group development, 150
    and personal development, 149
John, E., 46
Johnson, S.B., 38
joint ventures, 65
Jung, C., 210, 223-4
Juran, J.M., 200
just-in-time, 225

Kaltz, M., 33
Keller, H., 4

Kennedy, Pres. J.F., 13, 24, 47
Kentucky Fried Chicken, 5
kinaesthetic
    intelligence, 47-8
    state, 140
King, M.L., 10
kipper theory, 145
Kipling, R., 187
KISS technique, the, 73
knowing your negotiating opponent,
    102
Kolb, D., 16

Land, E., 75
language, the power of, 95-9
LATE mnemonic of coaching skills,
    the, 117-8
lateral thinking, 18-9
laughter, 193
lead-in-petrol issue, 161, 169
leadership,
    principle of interpersonal, 227
    principle of personal, 227
leading question, 99
learning
    and beliefs, integrated nature of,
        201-3
    centres, 173, 200
    cycle, 48
    log, 22, 48
    from mistakes, 199
    organisation, 199-200
    styles, 16-24, 116
        questionnaire, 20
learning,
    experiential, 16
    the four stages of, 24-7
        lessons from, 27
    incremental, 28
    lifelong, 12-3, 27, 34, 38, 196, 198-9,
        225
    objectives, 116
    new, 28
    transformational, 28-9
leasing, 65
Leeson, N., 230
legal environment, 58-9

Lenin, V.I., 2
Lewis, P.V., 181
licensing, 66
Liddon, H.P., 219
lifelong learning, 12-3, 27, 34, 38,
    198-9, 225
Likert's Four Systems of
    Management, 23
limited authority negotiation strategy,
    103
Lincoln, Pres. A., 2
linguistic intelligence, 46-8
listening skills, 117, 128
listening, reflective, 102, 123
locus of control, internal, 221
logical intelligence, 47-8
loss leaders, 179
Louganis, G., 40
Luft, J., 147

Macaulay, T.B., 159
McDonalds, 65
machines audit, 58
maintenance people, 151
maintenance, autonomous, 201
management
    buyouts, 66
    by wandering about (MBWA), 200
management,
    by exception (MBE), 73
    crisis, 19
    culture audit, 58
    expertise, poor, 230
    information systems (MIS),
        audit, 58
    inspirational, 55
    open-book, 199-200
    profile, 58
    structure, 228
        audit, 58
        poor, 230
    succession, 115, 126
Management, Likert's Four Systems
    of, 23
Managerial Grid, Blake and Mouton's,
    23
MANIA mnemonic for selection

    criteria, the, 120-1
manpower audit, 57
market
    development, 62
    penetration, 62
    positioning, 64
    segmentation, 64
    -share strategies, 64
    strategy (PIMS), profit impact of,
        69-70
Market Research Society, 165
marketing
    audit, 58
    competency, 224
    environment, 59
    and ethics, 179
    mix, 63-4, 224
    strategies, 63-4
Maslow, A., 214
Maslow's Hierarchy of Needs, 23
matching
    body movements, 141-2
    words, 139-41
materials audit, 57
maturity in selection, 121
Maxwell, R., 162
McDonalds, 170
media monitoring standards, the,
    166-7
meditation time, 144
meetings, 24, 105-10
    after, 107
    before, 106
    during, 106-7
    four P agenda for successful, 107-8
    group dynamics and, 108-9
    group roles at, 109-10
memory
    joggers, 48
    overload, 117
    skills, 24
MEMORY system for names, the,
    137-8, 249
mentoring, 16, 110-6, 225
    benefits of, 114-6
    relationships, 114
    system, 112-3

mergers, 66
Michelangelo, 2, 45
Milton, J., 4
mind
  and body one system, 191-2
  discipline, 232-4
  maps, 22, 45, 48
  programming the, 192-7
  reading in communication, 97
Mini car, 67
MISFILING mnemonic for company
failure factors, the, 229-32, 253
mission, 53-4, 57, 227
Missionaries of Charity, 211
Mitchell, M., 2
mnemonics, 48
money issues, 57
money,
  the importance of, 237-9
monitoring standards
  - animal welfare, 171-2
  - environmental groups, 170-1
  — the media, 166-7
  — the professions, 176-7
Moore, J.M., 164
moral blindness, group, 89
Morris Minor, 67
motivation
  for learning, 216
motivation, 213-5
  PURE SCRIBES mnemonic for
    sources of, 213-5
  in selection, 120
motivator coaching role, 119
motor-cycle industry, 230
movement intelligence, 47
movements,
  matching body, 141-2
  watching eye, 141
Mozart, W.A., 46
multiskilling, 200-1
musical intelligence, 46, 48
multiple intelligences, 45-9, 188
Mumford, A., 18, 20
mushroom theory, 145

names, the MEMORY system for

remembering, 137-8
natural
  aptitudes in selection, 121
  self in communication, being your,
    82
negative
  attitudes, 9, 12, 127, 191
  self-talk, 193, 210
  thinking, 36, 191
negotiation, 7, 10
  skills, basic, 100-3
  strategies, 103-5
Nestlé's infant formula, 167
neurolinguistic programming, 24
net present value (NPV)
Nicklaus, J., 40
Niebuhr, R., 40
Nixon, Pres. R., 146
Nobel Prize for Peace, 3
non-assertive behaviour, 42, 94
norming, group, 108-9
North Korea, 90
North Vietnam, 90
nuclear waste, 170
nullification of divergent views, group,
  89

objective-orientation, 57, 226
offshore accounts, 167
open (-ended) question, 99-100, 120
opening position in negotiation, 101
opportunism, freewheeling, 52
oppression, group, 89
optimum experience model, 209-10
options, 7
  people, 152
organic growth strategies, 61-2
organisational conflict, 91-2
others people, 152
outside-reference people, 151-2
overgearing, 231
overhead question, 100
ozone layer, 161, 170

PACE mnemonic on life issues, the,
  212-3
Palmer, R., 53

panic zone, the, 14-5
Paradise Lost, 4
Pareto principle, 23, 226
passion
  and enthusiasm, 207-8
  and success, 55
passive behaviour, 42, 94
pauses, 84
pay issues, 160
Peale, N.V., 36
Pearl Harbour, 89
Peck, M.S., 33
Pele, 207
people
  and meetings, 108
  the most important resource, 201
  people, 152
  and success, 56
Pepsi Cola, 67
perception in communication, 85-90
perceptual
  defence, 87
  readiness, 86
performance
  appraisal, 113, 123-7
  and meetings, 107
  potential model, 126
performing, group, 109
Persil, 67
persistence, 1-3, 27-8
personal
  development
    and comfort zones, 13-4
    and the Johari Window, 149
  differences, 91
  leadership, principle of, 227
  management, principle of, 227
  vision, principle of, 227
perspective, 211-3
PEST mnemonic, the, 58-9
Peters, T., 227
PEW mnemonic of mind dimensions,
  the, 192
Phosvel, 168
Picasso, P., 45
PICTURE mnemonic for

communicating, 82-3, 247
PIMS (profit impact of market
  strategy) model, 69-70
pitch in communication, 82
place in marketing, 63
placebo effect, 192
plan and success, 54-5
planning, 11
planning, lack of, 230
plant role, 109-10
plastic bags, 161
Plato, 46
Player, G., 47
POCKET mnemonic of negotiation
  process, the, 101
POETIC mnemonic of mentoring
  relationships, the, 114
Polaroid, 75
policy and meetings, 108
political environment, 58-9
Polly Peck, 229
Porter, M.E., 224
portfolio concept, 57
position
  audit, 57-8
  power, 163
  and success, 55-6
positive
  affirmations, 39, 193-6
  self-talk, 36, 39, 144, 210
  thinking, 36, 192-3, 239
Post-it notes, 75
posture, 39, 84, 142
power,
  abuse of, 160, 163
  and ethics, 162-3
  and motivation, 213
pragmatist learning, 17-9
  improving, 23-4
praise, 35, 38, 125
present, living in the, 144
presentation skills, 24, 225
Presley, E., 46, 186
pretence negotiation strategy, 104
price in marketing, 64
  -fixing, 161
  in marketing, 64

pricing and company failure, 231
principle and success, 5
privacy, right to, 160
prioritising, 226
proactive people, 151
proactivity, 19, 52, 226
problem solving, 23, 47, 93
procedures people, 151
product, 63
    development, 62
    differentiation, 64
    life cycle, 23, 58, 67-8, 224
    in marketing, 63
    and success, 55
production competence, 224-5
productivity through people, 228
professional standards, monitoring,
    176-7
profit
    impact of market strategy (PIMS),
        69-70
    and loss accounts, 67, 224
    objective, 53
    partnership, 231
    and success, 56
project work, 15-6, 226
promotion in marketing, 63
Prontoprint, 65
psychological barrier
PURE SCRIBES mnemonic for
    motivation sources, the, 213-5
purpose and success, 54
putting it all together, 243-55
Pygmalion effect, the, 186

qualifications in selection, 120
quality circles, 198-9, 201
question mark products, 69
question,
    factual, 99
    leading, 99
    marks potential, 127
    open, 99-100
    overhead, 100
    redirected, 100
    what if?, 102
questions, 23, 99-100, 117-8, 120-1

rapport, 137-54, 248-9
    with yourself, 143-5
    by remembering names, creating,
        137-8
rate of speech, 83
ratio analysis, 23
rationalisation, group, 89
reactive people, 19, 52, 151
recognition and motivation, 214
recruitment, 225
recurring pauses in communication,
    84
redirected question, 100
redundancy, 160
re-engineering, business process,
    29-30, 91, 224
Reeve, C., 4
reflection learning, 17
reflective listening, 102, 123
reflector learning, 17-9
    improving, 21-2
reflex intelligence, 47
reframing, 142-3
rehearsal, mental, 196-7
relationships, 233-4
relaxation time, 144
relevancy of learning, 215
Rembrandt, H, van R., 45
renewing, 226-7
resistance, overcoming, 5-7
respect and motivation, 214
restraining forces, 7-8
reward systems, 55, 93, 200
Rice Institute, A.K., 149
right first time, getting it, 197-8
rising stars potential, 126
risk
    aversion, 35
    and control, balance between, 228
Robbins, A., 81
role
    incompatibility, 90
    play, 16, 47
Roosevelt, E., 220

Saab, 63
St Augustine, 3

safety issues, 232
salami negotiation strategy, 103
Sanders, Col., 5
SAVER mnemonic for programming
    mind, the, 193-7, 250
and behaviour, 203
SCALD mnemonic of interview types,
    the, 119
SCAM mnemonic of coaching roles,
    the, 118-9
scarcity mentality, 37, 191
SCARE mnemonic of emotional IQ,
    the, 233-4, 253
S curve of progress, 28
Search of Excellence, In, 227
secondment, 16
sectarianism, 160
security and motivation, emotional,
    214
segregation, 160
selection
    interview, 119-21, 225
    issues, 160
self people, 152
self-
    acceptance, 36, 39, 145
    actualisation, 214
    censorship, 89
    confidence, 115
    control, 233
    development, 10-2, 22
    discipline, 219-21
        and wisdom, 221-3
    empowerment, 221
    enhancement, 43
    esteem, 33-49
        and assertiveness, 42-5
        characteristics,
            high, 36-9
            learning, 37-8
            positive thinking, 36-7
            relationships, 38-9
        enhancing your, 39-42
            external, 40-2
            internal, 39-40
        low, 35-6
        and motivation, 214

the SIMILAR mnemonic for, 45-7
fulfilling prophecy, 85, 185-6, 188,
    204
renewal, principle of balanced, 227
talk,
    constructive, 193-6
    negative, 193, 210
    positive, 36, 39, 144, 210
    worth, 34-5, 39, 144, 233
sensory perception, 233
serenity prayer, 40
Serious Fraud Office, 229
Seven Habits of Highly Effective
    People, 226
seven intelligences, lessons from, 48-9
sexism, 160, 179
sexual harassment, 160
Shakespeare, W., 47
shaper role, 109
share partnership, 228
shareholders, 53
Shaw, G.B., 17
Sheen enquiry, 169
short-termism, 230-1
SIMILAR mnemonic of abilities, the,
    45-7246
simplifying your life, 239
simulations, 16, 196
simultaneous loss-tight properties,
    228
Sinatra, F., 46
Singer Sewing Machines, 65
skills development, 115
SLANT mnemonic of body language,
    83
SLAPDASH mnemonic of negotiation
    strategies, the, 103-5
social
    environment, 59
    reporting, corporate, 177
Socrates, 46
solidarity, group, 89
Sony Walkman, 144
spatial intelligence, 45, 48
SPECIFIC mnemonic of group roles,
    the, 109-10
speed reading, 24

sperm, 39
SPEWSIC mnemonic of strategic
    planning, the, 56-76, 247
spirituality, 204
sponsor mentoring role, 112
Spooner, P., 163
sports
    psychologists, 196
    sponsorship, 179
staff turnover, 115
stakeholder
    issues, 160-1
    theory, 180
stakeholders, 52-3
    and ethics, 179-80
stamina, 3-4
standard practice negotiation
strategy, 103
standards,
    double, 43, 168-9
    monitoring
    — animal welfare, 171-2
    — environmental groups, 170-1
    — the media, 166-7
    — the professions, 176-7
star products, 68
stereotyping, 87
sticking to the knitting, 228
storming, group, 108
STORMING mnemonic, 89
strain zone, the, 14-5
strategic
    alliances, 65
    objectives, 172
    planning, advantages of, 73-4
    thinking, 51-79, 246-7
strategies,
    acquisition, 62-3
    business, 65-6
    marketing, 63-4
    organic growth, 61-2
stress, 123, 192, 237
    environmental, 91
stretch zone, the, 14-5
strokes for different folks, different,
    150-2
structures, divisionalised, 55

submissive behaviour, 42, 94
success, core skills for business, 224-5
suggestion schemes, 198-9
SUPPORT mnemonic of habits for
    effective living, the, 226-7
supporter coaching role, 118
SWOT analysis, 11, 59, 74
synergising, 226
systems thinking, 18

task people, 151
tax
    evasion, 167
    issues, 232
Taylorite view, 198
team building, 93
teamwork, 200-1, 231
technological environment, 59
Teets, J.W., 51
Teresa, Mother, 211
terminating negotiation, 103
territorial instinct, 90
theorist learning, 17-9
    improving, 22-3
things people, 152
thinking win-win, 227
time management, 47
Toastmasters, 47
tobacco industry, 167-8
tone of voice, 82-3
TOPMOST mnemonic of behaviour
    styles, the, 150-2
total quality management (TQM), 198,
    224
towards people, 150
toxic waste, 161, 181
trainer mentoring role, 112
training, 45, 114-5, 125, 200, 202
transactional analysis (TA), 24, 42
transformational learning, 28-9
transparency, 166, 176
TRAP mnemonic on learning styles,
    the, 18-9
TRIPE mnemonic on interpersonal
    conflict, the, 90-2
trust
    control dilemma, the, 147

trust,
    building, 145-6
Twain, M., 1

unconscious
    competence, 26-7, 203
    incompetence, 25
understanding in communication, 83
understanding,
    the habit of, 226
    testing, 118
unfair competition, 161
unlearning, 28
Union Carbide, 167-8
UNIT model of learning, the, 27-9
    lessons from, 29-30
United States Postal service (USPS),
    232
unspecified verbs and nouns, 96-7

values, 10, 91, 97-9, 172, 203-4, 227
    -driven culture, 227
    and perception, 85-6
Van Buren, A., 221
variance analysis, 23
Velsicol Chemical Co., 168-9
venturing, corporate, 66
vertical diversification, 62-3
vision, 10, 53, 227
    statement, 54, 57, 172, 227
visual state, 139-40
visualisation, 17, 45, 102
    of success, 196
voice in communication, 84, 142

Volkswagen Beetle, 67
Volvo, 170
voodoo effect, 191

waste disposal management, 161
Waterford Glass, 63, 228
Watergate scandal, 146, 166
Waterman, R., 227
Wharton School of Business, 53
what if? questions, 102
wild-cat products, 69
will-power, 5, 45
Winfrey, O., 46
win-win, 93, 95, 101, 103, 227
win and motivation, the urge to, 214
wisdom, 221-4
Wogan, T., 46
words of
    necessity, 99
    possibility, 98
working conditions, 160
world class manufacturing, 225
World Health Organisation, 168
wots up analysis, 59-61
    external, 60-1
    internal, 60
Wright brothers, 76

XtraVision, 229

Yeager, C., 190
Yeats, W.B., 223

zero defects, 197-8